Embellishments A to Z

An Embellishment Idea Book

Embellishments A to Z

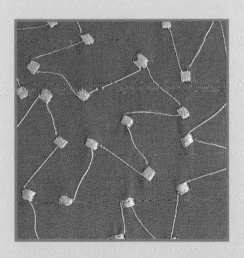

STEPHANIE VALLEY

The Taunton Press

Publisher
Jim Childs

Acquisitions Editor
Jolynn Gower

Editorial Assistant
Sarah Coe

Copy Editor
Candace B. Levy

Designer/Layout Artist
Lisa Sloane

Interior Photographer
Nathan Ham

Cover photographer
Scott Phillips

Illustrator
Ronald Carboni

The Taunton Press

Printed in Singapore
10 9 8 7 6 5 4 3 2 1

The Taunton Press, Inc.
63 South Main Street, PO Box 5506
Newtown, CT 06470-5506
e-mail: tp@taunton.com
Distributed by Publishers Group West

Library of Congress Cataloging-in-Publication Data
Valley, Stephanie.
Embellishments A to Z / Stephanie Valley.
p.   cm.
"An embellishment idea book."
ISBN 1-56158-307-3
1. Fancy work. 2. Machine sewing. I. Title
TT751.V27   1999
746—dc21   99-20155
CIP

To my wonderful husband, John. Many thanks for your encouragement and support and most of all for always bringing a smile to my face. Special thanks also to our first child who was a good baby and allowed me to have a happy and healthy pregnancy while working on this project.

Contents

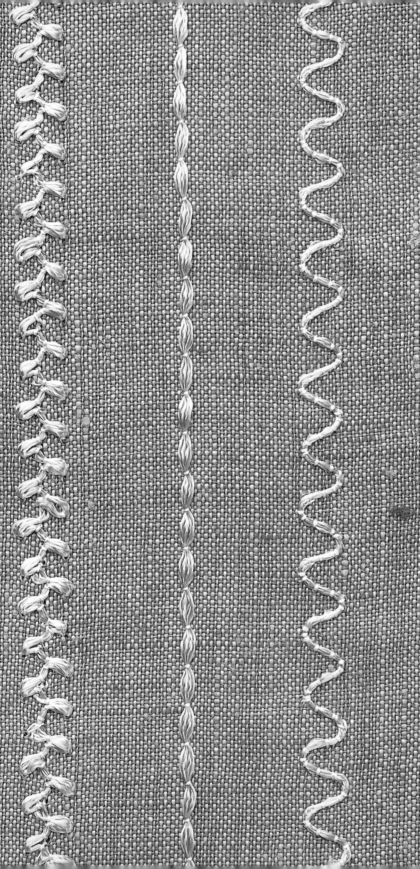

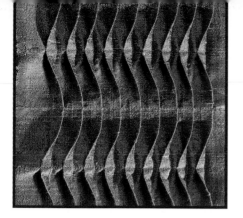
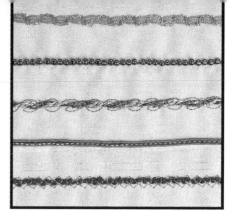

Introduction

CRAFTSWORKERS HAVE BEEN ENHANCING THEIR PRODUCTS WITH embellishments for centuries. Details make a statement about an object's purpose, recipient, or creator. Because time is in short supply in our modern society, embellishments are often overlooked. We are often rushing just to finish a project, much less allowing ourselves time to add creative details.

Use this simple and concise reference guide as a starting point, and make time to experiment. Allow yourself the freedom to expand your horizon of knowledge and to explore a process without feeling compelled to create a finished "thing." Not everyone is excited by machine embroidery, fringing, stenciling, or devoré. But techniques you never before thought to try might offer new inspiration, turning a cookie-cutter project into an original creation. Ideas form and grow only out of opportunity.

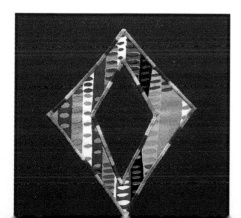

Appliqué

APPLIQUÉ IS THE STITCHING OF CUTOUT FABRIC SHAPES onto another fabric. Cutout designs can be joined to fabric in a variety of methods, including basic fused appliqué, reverse appliqué, padded appliqué, and shadow appliqué, depending on the desired look. Fused appliqué is a quick-and-easy technique that works best with lightweight to medium-weight fabrics that can withstand the heat of fusing. Reverse appliqué requires stable fabrics and has a softer finished hand than does fused appliqué because there are fewer layers of fabric. Padded appliqué adds dimension and is created with low-loft quilt batting, polyester fleece, or felt. Transparent fabrics—such as batiste, handkerchief linen, organdy, and organza—give shadow appliqué its subtle, delicate appearance.

Basic
Fused Appliqué

EASY

SUPPLIES

FILE FOLDER FOR TEMPLATE

FUSIBLE WEB

CHALK MARKER OR NO. 2
   PENCIL

TEAR-AWAY STABILIZER

EMBROIDERY FOOT

MACHINE EMBROIDERY OR
   RAYON THREAD

BOBBINFIL

1   Prepare a paper template of the design.

2   Cut a piece of fusible web slightly larger than the design.

3   Press the nonpaper side of the fusible web to the wrong side of the appliqué fabric, following the manufacturer's instructions.

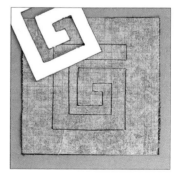

4   Place the template, wrong side up, on the fusible web's paper backing. Using a chalk marker or no. 2 pencil, trace the design onto the paper.

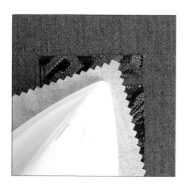

5   Cut out the appliqué design.

6   Remove the paper backing from the fusible web. Position the appliqué on the right side of the base fabric. Fuse the appliqué into place, following the manufacturer's instructions.

7 Cut a piece of tear-away stabilizer 1 in. to 2 in. larger than the appliqué. Position the stabilizer under the base fabric. Pin the stabilizer in place. (Use additional layers of stabilizer as necessary.)

8 Place the embroidery foot in the sewing machine. Thread the needle with embroidery thread, and use Bobbinfil in the bobbin.

9 Set the machine for a narrow (³/₄ mm), short (1 mm) zigzag. Position the raw edge of the fabric under the center of the embroidery foot. Stitch around the outside edges of the appliqué.

10 Set the machine for a 1¹/₂-mm- to 5-mm-wide satin stitch, depending on desired look. Stitch around the outside edges of the appliqué, covering the previous zigzag stitching.

11 Remove the tear-away stabilizer.

❖ STITCHING OUTSIDE CORNERS—Sew past the corner half as far as the stitches are wide. Stop with the needle down in the fabric on the outside swing of the zigzag. Pivot the fabric, and continue stitching, sewing over the previous stitching at the corner.

❖ STITCHING INSIDE CORNERS—Sew past the corner half as far as the stitches are wide. Stop with the needle down in the fabric on the inside swing of the zigzag. Pivot the fabric, and continue stitching, sewing over the previous stitching at the corner.

Reverse Appliqué

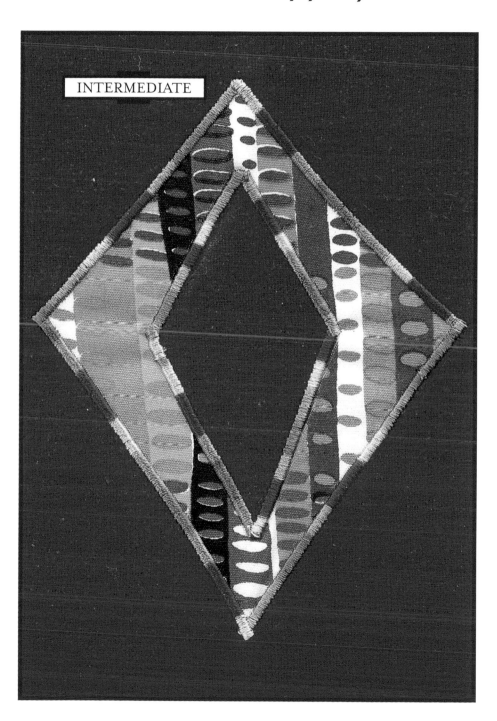

INTERMEDIATE

SUPPLIES

File folder for template

Chalk marker or

    no. 2 pencil

Tear-away stabilizer

Fusible interfacing

    (optional)

Embroidery hoop

    (optional)

Embroidery foot

Machine embroidery or

    rayon thread

Bobbinfil

Appliqué scissors

1   Prepare a paper template of the design.

2   Place the template, wrong side down, on the right side of the base fabric. Using a chalk marker or no. 2 pencil, trace the design onto the fabric.

3   Cut a piece of tear-away stabilizer and a piece of appliqué fabric slightly larger than the design. Optional: Cut a piece of lightweight fusible interfacing slightly larger than the design. Following the manufacturer's instructions, fuse the interfacing to the wrong side of the base fabric under the traced design.

4   With the right side up, center the appliqué fabric and stabilizer under the traced design. Pin the layers together. Optional: An embroidery hoop can be used to keep the layers together and taut.

5   Place the embroidery foot in the sewing machine. Thread the needle with embroidery thread, and use Bobbinfil in the bobbin.

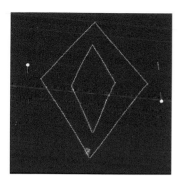

6 Set the machine for a narrow (¾ mm), short (1 mm) zigzag. With the base fabric right side up, stitch along the design lines through all three layers.

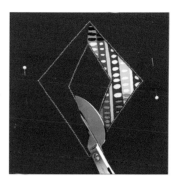

7 With the right side up, use appliqué scissors to cut away the base fabric from inside the stitching lines.

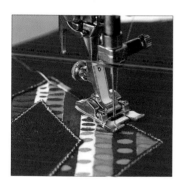

8 Set the machine for a 1½- to 5-mm-wide satin stitch, depending on the desired look. Place the raw edge of the fabric under the center of the embroidery foot. Stitch around the edges of the appliqué, covering the previous zigzag stitching.

9 Trim away the extra appliqué fabric, and remove the stabilizer.

❖ STITCHING POINTS—Sew just past the point and stop with the needle down in the fabric. Pivot the fabric 90 degrees, and sew to cover the previous stitching. Stop with the needle down in fabric on the outside edge. Pivot the fabric, and continue stitching.

❖ FELTED WOOLS, KNITS, AND COATINGS produce interesting reverse appliqués; and because they don't fray, they require no satin stitching to finish.

Padded Appliqué

INTERMEDIATE

SUPPLIES

FILE FOLDER FOR TEMPLATE

TEAR-AWAY STABILIZER

CHALK MARKER OR
   NO. 2 PENCIL

LOW-LOFT QUILT BATTING,
   POLYESTER FLEECE, OR FELT

EMBROIDERY FOOT

MACHINE EMBROIDERY OR
   RAYON THREAD

BOBBINFIL

APPLIQUÉ SCISSORS

EMBROIDERY HOOP
   (OPTIONAL)

1   Prepare a paper template of the design.

2   Cut a piece of tear-away stabilizer I in. to 2 in. larger than the design.

3   Place the template, wrong side up, on the stabilizer. Using a chalk marker or no. 2 pencil, trace the design onto the stabilizer.

4   Position the stabilizer on the wrong side of the base fabric. Pin in place.

5   Cut a piece of batting and a piece of appliqué fabric slightly larger than the design.

6   With right sides up, center the batting and appliqué fabric on right side of the base fabric over the design area. Pin in place from the wrong side of the base fabric. Optional: Use an embroidery hoop to keep the layers together.

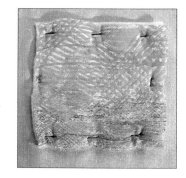

7 Place the embroidery foot in the sewing machine. Thread the needle with embroidery thread, and use Bobbinfil in the bobbin.

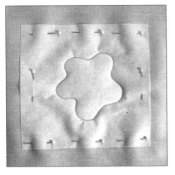

8 Set the machine for a 1-mm straight stitch. With the wrong side of the base fabric up, stitch along the design lines through all layers.

9 Using appliqué scissors, trim away the extra batting and appliqué fabric close to the stitching.

10 Set the machine for a 2-mm- to 5-mm-wide satin stitch, depending on the desired look. Stitch around the outside edges of the appliqué, covering the previous straight stitching.

11 Remove the stabilizer.

❖ STITCHING AROUND CURVES — Stop with the needle down in the fabric on the outside edge of the curve. Raise the embroidery foot, and slightly pivot the fabric. Continue stitching. Repeat the process around the curve as needed.

Shadow Appliqué

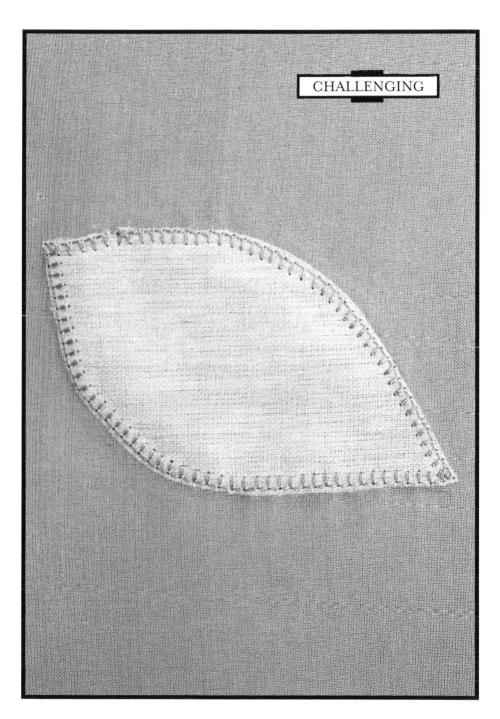

CHALLENGING

SUPPLIES

FILE FOLDER FOR TEMPLATE

SPRAY STABILIZER

WATER-SOLUBLE MARKER OR

    NO. 2 PENCIL

WATER-SOLUBLE STABILIZER

EMBROIDERY HOOP

70/9 NEEDLE

EMBROIDERY FOOT

MACHINE EMBROIDERY OR

    RAYON THREAD

BOBBINFIL

APPLIQUÉ SCISSORS

1   Prewash all fabrics.

2   Prepare a paper template of the design.

3   Apply a medium coat of spray stabilizer to the right side of the base fabric in the design area and to the appliqué fabric.

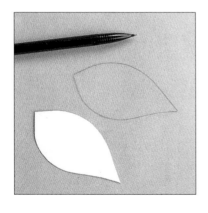

4   Place the template, right side up, on the right side of the base fabric. Trace the design onto the fabric using a water-soluble marker or no. 2 pencil.

5   Cut a piece of water-soluble stabilizer and a piece of appliqué fabric slightly larger than the design and embroidery hoop.

6   With right sides up, layer the stabilizer and appliqué fabric under the design area of the base fabric. Pin the layers together.

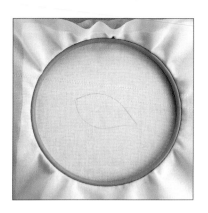

7   With right sides up, insert the fabric
    layers into the embroidery hoop. To
    do this, lay the fabric, right sides up,
    on top of outer ring; then insert the
    inner ring and tighten the screw.
    The fabric should be tight, like a
    drum, in the hoop. Remove the pins.

8   Place the embroidery foot and a
    70/9 needle in the sewing machine.
    Thread the needle with embroidery
    thread, and use Bobbinfil in the
    bobbin. Set the machine for a short
    straight stitch. Do not start at a cor-
    ner. Draw the bobbin thread up to
    the top. Sew a few stitches to secure.
    Change the machine setting to a
    decorative stitch, such as blind-

hemming or blanket stitch. Adjust the width and length to the
desired setting; the straight edge of the stitch should fall on the
design line, and the swing of the needle should go into the
appliqué. Stitch along the design lines through all layers. Secure
with straight stitching at the end.

9   Using appliqué scissors, trim the
    excess appliqué fabric and stabilizer
    from the wrong side.

10 Remove the remaining stabilizer by
    soaking it in warm water.

Bias Binding

BIAS BINDING IS A STRIP OF FABRIC CUT AT A 45-DEGREE angle to the selvage. Bias-cut fabric is used for binding because it is more flexible and easier to shape around curves than is fabric cut along the straight grain or crossgrain. Knit fabric is the exception to the rule and has the most stretch along the crossgrain. Binding strips are stitched to and wrapped around a raw edge of another fabric. This technique is often used as a decorative seam or hem for garments and as a finish for quilts. Single and double binding are the two basic methods of application. Single binding is suitable for most fabrics; double binding works best with lightweight to medium-weight fabrics, because more layers of fabric are involved.

Single Binding

INTERMEDIATE

1   Cut bias strips four times the desired finished width of binding plus ¼ in. to ⅜ in. to allow for wrapping and stretching. Join strips to create the length of binding needed for the project.

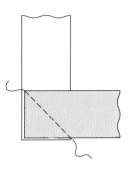

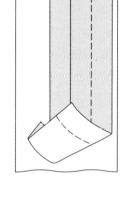

2   With wrong sides together, fold the binding in half lengthwise, and press lightly.

3   Open out the binding strip, and fold the raw edges toward the center crease. Press lightly.

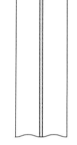

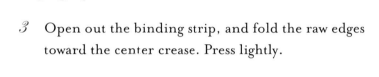

4   Open out the binding strip. With right sides together and raw edges even, pin the binding to the base fabric. Then stitch along the first crease line.

5   Wrap the binding over the raw edges of the seam allowance to meet the stitching line. Pin in place, and slipstitch over the seamline.

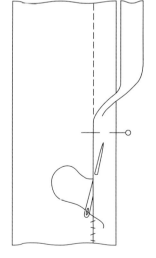

Double Binding

INTERMEDIATE

1 Cut bias strips six times the desired finished width of the binding plus ¼ in. to ⅜ in. to allow for wrapping and stretching. Join strips to create the length of binding needed for the project.

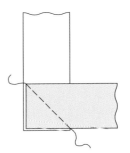

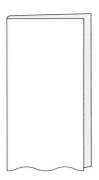

2 With wrong sides together, fold the binding in half lengthwise, and press lightly.

3 With right sides together and raw edges even, pin the binding to the base fabric. Stitch together, using a seam allowance that is slightly less than the desired finished width of the binding.

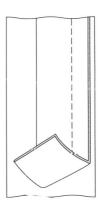

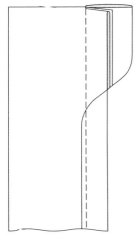

4 Lightly press the binding away from the base fabric. Wrap the binding over the raw edges of the seam allowance to just cover the stitching line. Pin in place, and slipstitch over the seam line; or baste in place, and machine topstitch in the ditch from the right side.

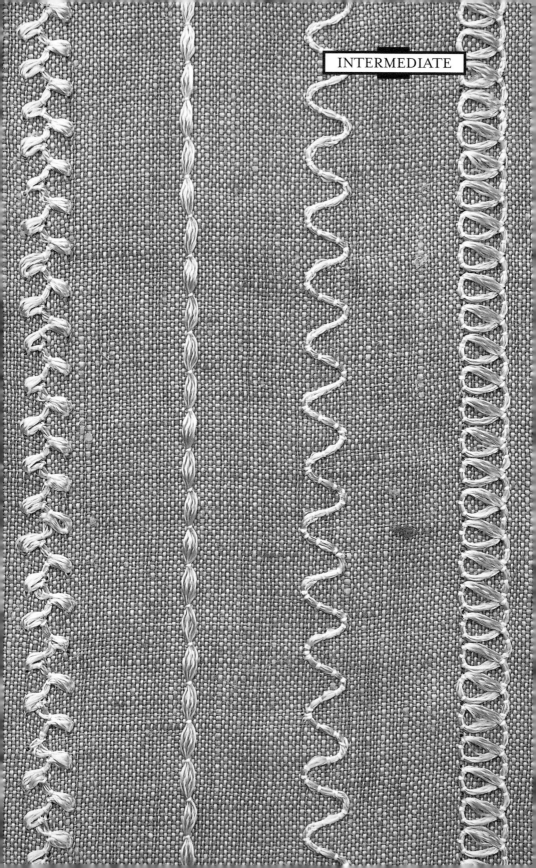

CHAPTER 3

Bobbin Work

SPECIALTY THREADS MAY BE USED IN THE BOBBIN TO create a variety of decorative effects and embellishments. Stitching is done with the right side of the fabric facing down. Many threads too heavy to be used as a needle thread, such as pearl cotton, ribbon floss, and metallic thread, produce exciting results when used in the bobbin. Threads can be wound slowly onto the bobbin by hand or on the sewing machine if you bypass the tension disk. Decorative stitch patterns can accommodate heavier threads with a slight adjustment of preset lengths and widths. Apply bobbin work as an accent on pillow tops, holiday projects, and shirt collars and cuffs.

SUPPLIES

Decorative thread or ribbon

Extra bobbin case (Black latch)

Cotton embroidery or nylon monofilament thread

Tear-away stabilizer

Chalk marker

Large-eye needle (optional)

1 Wind the decorative thread onto the bobbin. This can be accomplished by hand or on the machine by leaving the thread out of the tension stud and winding at a slow speed.

2 Insert the bobbin into the extra bobbin case, and adjust the tension until the thread pulls freely from the case.

3 Insert the bobbin into the sewing machine, and thread the needle with cotton embroidery thread.

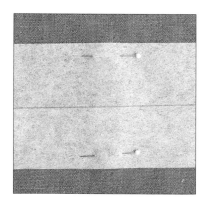

4 Mark a stitching line or trace a mirror image of a design onto tear-away stabilizer. Pin or baste the stabilizer to the wrong side of the fabric.

5   Insert the fabric into the machine with the wrong side up, and place a second layer of fabric or tear-away stabilizer on top.

6   Select a straight stitch with a length between 3 mm and 4 mm or a decorative stitch. Stitch a sample, and adjust the bobbin and needle tensions as needed. Stitch slowly for best results. Do not backstitch at the beginning or end.

7   Remove the stabilizer.

❖ **IF THE BOBBIN WORK does not end in a seam, use a large-eye needle to pull the thread ends to the wrong side of the fabric. Knot the ends, and trim.**

❖ **DO NOT USE A STANDARD BOBBIN CASE for bobbin work. The tension adjustment will affect the stitching when using regular sewing thread. Mark the special bobbin case with dab of fingernail polish.**

❖ **TIGHTEN THE NEEDLE TENSION for straight-stitch bobbin work.**

❖ **A SINGLE LAYER OF FABRIC can be stabilized with fusible interfacing, or muslin can be used as a second layer of fabric.**

CHAPTER 4

Couching

DECORATIVE THREADS, RIBBONS, YARNS, AND TRIMS CAN be attached to fabric by couching over them with a variety of machine stitches. Couching can add texture and dimension to all types of sewing projects, from quilts to fine garments. The securing stitches can be decorative by sewing with a contrasting thread or hidden by using matching thread or invisible monofilament thread. Open stitches that allow the couched thread or hem to show are the most interesting. Special cording and braiding feet are available for the sewing machine and are helpful in guiding the threads and producing precise results. Select a foot that is compatible with the number and size of threads and with the design.

Basic Couching

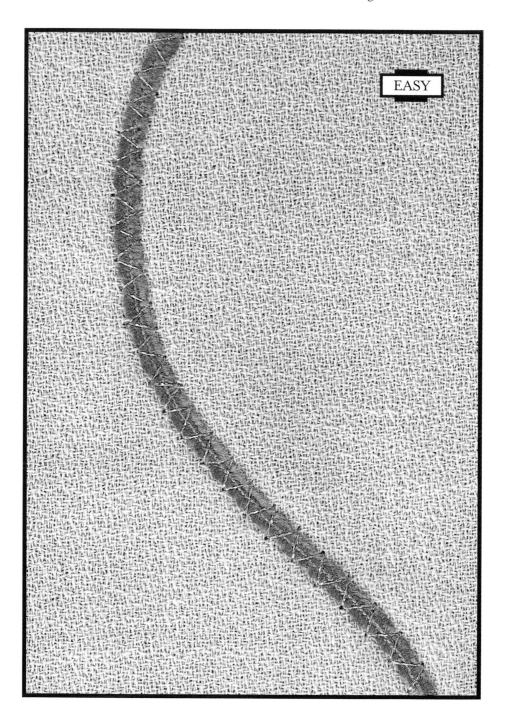

EASY

SUPPLIES

Chalk marker

Tear-away stabilizer

Decorative threads, cords, or ribbons

Braiding or cording foot

Bobbinfil

Embroidery, rayon, metallic, or mono-filament thread for stitching

Large-eye needle (optional)

1 Using a chalk marker, trace a stitching line or design onto the right side of the fabric.

2 Cut a piece of tear-away stabilizer slightly larger than the design. Position the stabilizer under the design on the fabric. Pin in place.

3 Insert the decorative thread through the opening in the front of the foot. If you are using multiple cords, knot the ends together. Attach the braiding or cord-ing foot to the sewing machine. Thread the needle with embroidery thread, and use Bobbinfil in the bobbin.

4 Select a stitch, and adjust the width to cover the decorative thread. Stitch slowly for best results. (The couching stitch shown in the sample is a 4-mm-wide, 2.5-mm-long zigzag.)

5 Remove the stabilizer.

6 If you are following a design motif or not ending in a seam, use a large-eye needle to pull the ends to the wrong side of the fabric. Knot the ends, and trim (see page 25).

❖ **COUCHED THREAD ENDS** can be finished with a small satin stitch and left to hang as a small tassel.

❖ **CROSS-LOCKED BEADS** can be secured at the beginning and end by removing several beads and knotting the thread ends together. Use a large-eye needle to pull the ends to the wrong side of the fabric.

VARIATIONS

A. DECORATIVE STITCH OVER
   CHENILLE THREAD
   Braiding foot
   Needle thread: rayon
      embroidery
   Bobbin thread: Bobbinfil
   Stitch length: 3 mm
   Stitch width: 5 mm

B. STRAIGHT STITCH
   THROUGH SOUTACHE BRAID
   Braiding foot
   Needle thread: rayon sulky
   Bobbin thread: Bobbinfil
   Stitch length: 2.5 mm
   Stitch width: 0

C. DECORATIVE STITCH OVER
   MULTIPLE CORDS
   Braiding foot
   Needle thread: cotton embroidery

Bobbin thread: Bobbinfil
Stitch length: 3 mm
Stitch width: 5 mm

D. UNIVERSAL STITCH OVER CROSS-
   LOCKED BEADS
   Tricot or Bulky Overlock foot
   Needle thread: monofilament
      thread
   Bobbin thread: Bobbinfil
   Stitch length: 2.5 mm
   Stitch width: 4 mm

E. DECORATIVE STITCH OVER
   1/8-IN. RIBBON
   Braiding foot
   Needle thread: variegated metallic
   Bobbin thread: Bobbinfil
   Stitch length: satin
   Stitch width: 5 mm

Twisted Thread Couching

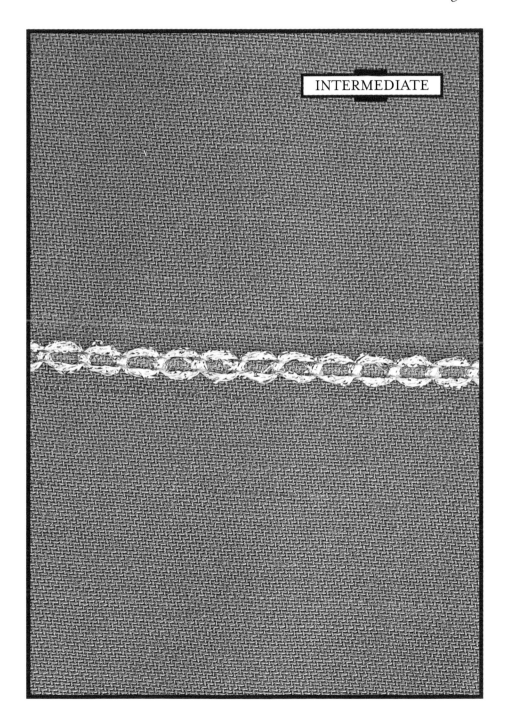

INTERMEDIATE

SUPPLIES

DECORATIVE THREADS, CORDS,
OR RIBBONS

CHALK MARKER

TEAR-AWAY STABILIZER

80 TWIN NEEDLE

OPEN-TOE EMBROIDERY FOOT

EMBROIDERY, RAYON, METAL-
LIC, OR MONOFILAMENT
THREAD FOR STITCHING

BOBBINFIL

LARGE-EYE NEEDLE
(OPTIONAL)

1 Cut the decorative threads three times the length needed for the design or stitching line.

2 Using a chalk marker, trace the stitching line or design onto the right side of the fabric.

3 Cut a piece of tear-away stabilizer slightly larger than the design. Position the stabilizer under the design on the fabric. Pin in place.

4 Place the twin needle and open-toe embroidery foot in the sewing machine. Thread the needle with embroidery thread, and use Bobbinfil in the bobbin.

5 Sink the needle into the right side of the base fabric. Wrap the center of the decorative threads around the back of the needle.

6 Set the machine for a 2-mm- to 5-mm-long straight stitch. Take two stitches, and sink the needle into the fabric. Crisscross the threads in front of needle. Take two stitches, and sink the needle into the fabric. Repeat these steps until the design is complete.

7 Remove the stabilizer.

8 If you are following a design motif or not ending in a seam, use a large-eye needle to pull the ends to the wrong side of the fabric. Knot the ends, and trim (see page 25).

❖ SOME MACHINE MODELS can be programmed to stop with the needle down after a set number of stitches.

❖ EXPERIMENT WITH THE STITCH LENGTH and the number of stitches between crisscrosses.

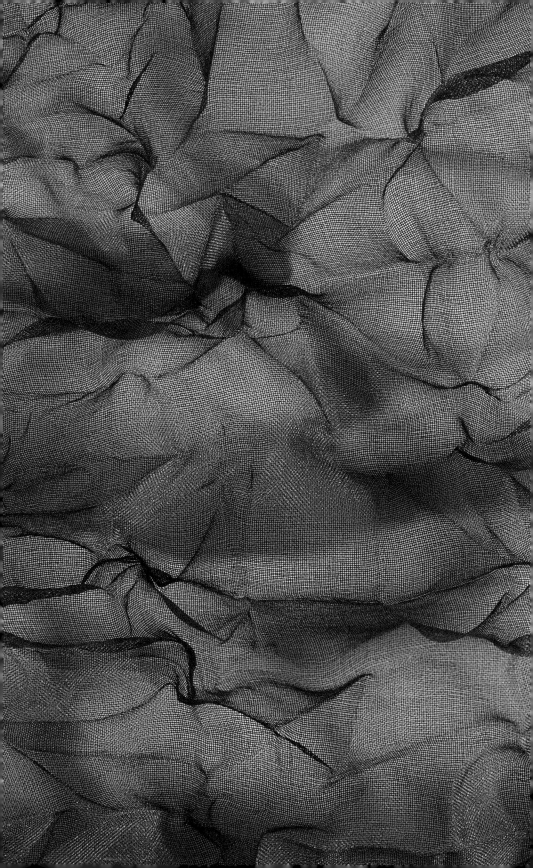

5

Crinkling

CRINKLING IS A SIMPLE METHOD FOR ADDING SURFACE texture to fabric. Lightweight natural-fiber fabrics crinkle most easily. Heavier fabrics are not as compressed in the crinkling process and, therefore, produce less texture. Synthetic fabrics are not candidates for crinkling because they do not hold a press. Damp fabric is twisted into a ball, secured, and heat-set in the dryer. The twisting gives an interesting, irregular wrinkled texture to the fabric. The texture, however, is not permanent; and the crinkling must be re-created after each washing. Between launderings, store the fabric in a ball. Simple accessories and pull-on garments are particularly suited to being crinkled. Fusible interfacing and/or decorative stitching can be added to crinkled fabric to secure the texture in place.

Basic Crinkling

EASY

1   Determine the amount of desired finished crinkled fabric. Add extra length and width to allow for the crinkling process.

SUPPLIES

COTTON STRING

PANTYHOSE FOOT

LIGHTWEIGHT FUSIBLE INTER-
    FACING (OPTIONAL)

2   Submerge the fabric in lukewarm water until thoroughly saturated.

3   Remove the fabric and squeeze out the excess water.

4   Fold the fabric in half lengthwise several times until it forms a narrow strip.

5   Twist the ends of the strip in opposite directions. The fabric should form a tight roll and begin to curl onto itself.

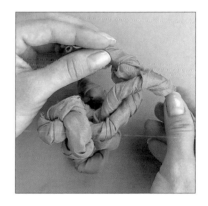

6   Continue twisting until the fabric roll forms a ball.

7   Secure the ball with cotton string. Tuck the ends of the fabric into the ball.

8 Place the secured ball into the toe of an old pair of pantyhose; knot the open end.

9 Place the fabric ball in the dryer along with several towels to buffer the noise and absorb the moisture. Tumble in a warm dryer until all the moisture has evaporated.

10 Remove the pantyhose and string from the ball and unwind the fabric.

11 Use as is or fuse and/or stitch to make the crinkles permanent.

❖ FABRIC MAY ALSO BE DRIED in a low-heat (200°F) oven to avoid dryer scuff marks. Do not leave the fabric in the oven unattended.

VARIATION 1

FUSING CRINKLED FABRIC

1   Place the crinkled fabric right side down on a pressing surface.

2   Stretch the fabric to the desired size, and pin in place.

3   Cut interfacing to the size needed. Place the fusible side of the interfacing down on the crinkled fabric.

4   Fuse into place following the manufacturer's instructions.

VARIATION 2

♦ After fusing the crinkled fabric to the interfacing, embellish the textured surface with beading and/or stitching.

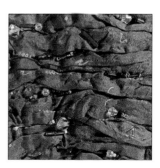

Crinkling with a Fabric Press

EASY

SUPPLIES

COTTON STRING
FABRIC PRESS

1 Determine the amount of desired finished crinkled fabric. Add extra length and width to allow for the crinkling process.

2 Press the fabric in half lengthwise several times until it forms a narrow strip.

3 Twist or wad the fabric into a ball.

4 Secure with cotton string, and tuck the ends of the fabric into the ball.

5 Set the fabric press to the appropriate setting for the fabric; do not use steam.

6 Place the fabric ball in the press. Heat several times, turning the pressed fabric ball to a different side each time.

7 Remove the ball from the press, and unwind the fabric.

Cutwork

CUTWORK IS AN EMBROIDERY TECHNIQUE THAT INVOLVES trimming away sections of a design that have been outlined with satin stitch. This delicate and ornate method has been used for centuries to embellish table linens, clothing, and accessories. The thread used for the satin stitching and the bars traditionally matches the base fabric or is a shade or two darker. Stitching is made easier if the complete design fits into an embroidery hoop. A distinguishing feature of cutwork is the bridges or bars that span the cutout areas and prevent the motifs from collapsing. Space the connecting bars at frequent intervals so the design has adequate stability. Finely woven fabrics that do not fray, such as linen and cotton, produce the best results.

SUPPLIES

FILE FOLDER FOR TEMPLATE
WATER-SOLUBLE STABILIZER
TEAR-AWAY STABILIZER
WATER-SOLUBLE MARKER
COTTON OR RAYON
    EMBROIDERY THREAD

75/11 EMBROIDERY NEEDLE
BOBBINFIL
APPLIQUÉ SCISSORS
OPEN-TOE EMBROIDERY
    FOOT

1   Prewash all the fabrics. Prepare a paper template of the design.

2   Cut a piece of water-soluble stabilizer, tear-away stabilizer, and secondary fabric slightly larger than the design.

3   Trace the design onto the water-soluble stabilizer using a water-soluble marker.

4   Sandwich the secondary fabric in between the tear-away stabilizer and the wrong side of the base fabric.

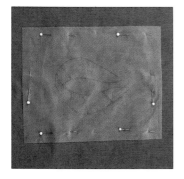

5   Place the water-soluble stabilizer on top of the right side of the base fabric. Pin all four layers of fabric and stabilizer together.

6   Use a 1.5-mm-long straight stitch and a 75/11 needle. Use embroidery thread in the needle and Bobbinfil in the bobbin. Stitch along all design lines.

7   With the wrong side of the base fabric facing up, use appliqué scissors to trim the tear-away stabilizer and both layers of fabric from the open areas of the design. Do not cut the water-soluble stabilizer from the open areas. Trim as close and neatly as possible.

8   With the right side of the base fabric facing up, use appliqué scissors to trim the water-soluble stabilizer from outside the design lines.

9   Place the embroidery foot in machine, and set the machine for a 2-mm-wide satin stitch. Stitch the connecting bars and small areas first; then stitch along the design outline. Cover the previous stitching and the raw edges of the fabric. Additional layers of water-soluble stabilizer may be placed under the

design when satin stitching. Pull the threads to the wrong side of fabric and knot.

10 With the wrong side of the fabric up, use appliqué scissors and trim the tear-away stabilizer and second layer of fabric from outside the design lines.

11 Soak the fabric in warm water to remove any remaining stabilizer. Press from the wrong side.

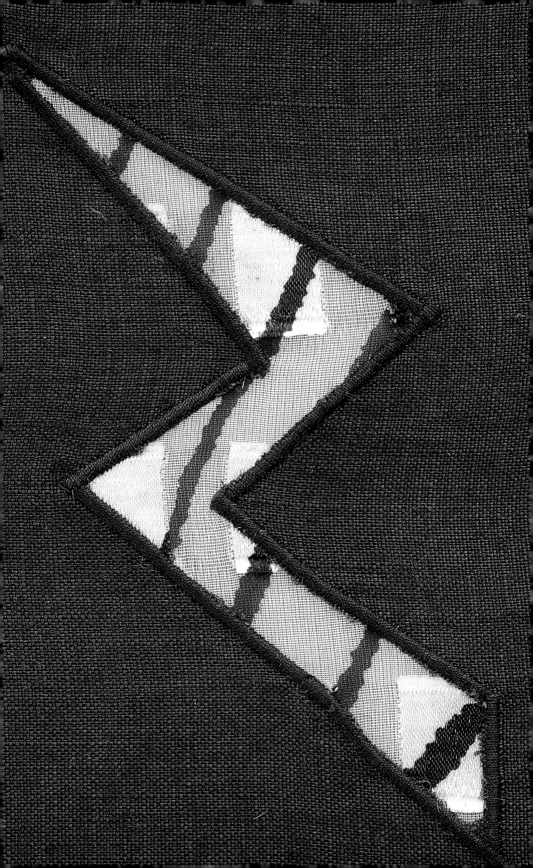

CHAPTER 7

Devoré

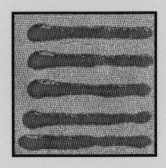

DEVORÉ IS A PROCESS OF REMOVING FIBERS FROM A FABRIC. Fiber-Etch is a commercial product that destroys cellulose (cotton, linen, and rayon) fibers. This pastelike substance is nontoxic and can be applied directly to the fabric with a squeeze bottle, nylon or foam brush, or rubber stamp. You can create a freehand design or use a silk screen, stencil, or paper template. A thin layer of Fiber-Etch is all that is needed to remove the fibers. A heavy application takes a long time to dry and is unnecessary. Once the product is dry, it is heated with a dry iron and then rinsed under running water, which removes the cellulose fibers. Devoré is an excellent surface embellishment for scarves and accessories. Fiber-Etch can also be used to create reverse appliqué and cutwork.

Devoré on Velvet

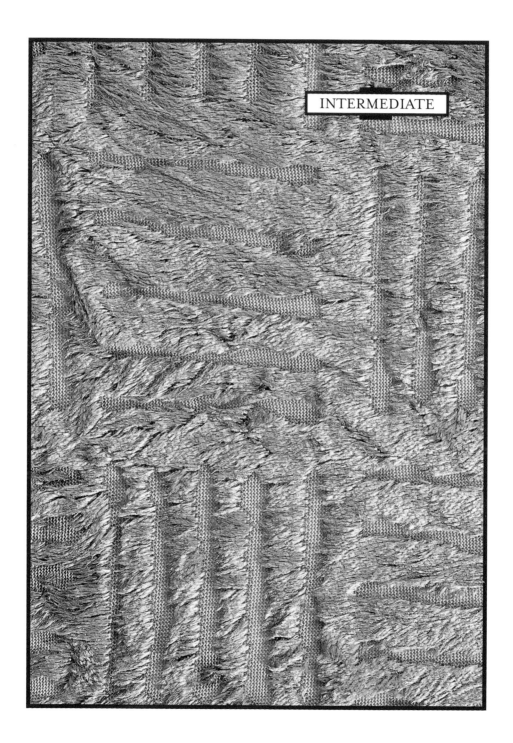

INTERMEDIATE

SUPPLIES

Chalk or water-soluble   Hair dryer
marker (optional)   Velva or needle board
Rayon-silk blend velvet   Press cloth (#20)
Fiber-Etch

1 If you'd like, use chalk or a water-soluble marker to trace the design onto the wrong side of the velvet.

2 With the wrong side of the velvet up, use the squeeze bottle to apply a thin layer of Fiber-Etch along the design lines or use the Fiber-Etch to create a freehand design.

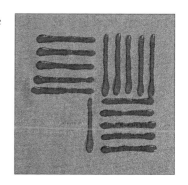

3 Dry the Fiber-Etch with a hair dryer.

4 Preheat a dry iron to the wool setting.

5 Place the velvet right side down on top of the Velva board. Place a press cloth over the design, and press the design area until the Fiber-Etch turns light brown and becomes brittle.

6   Rinse the fabric under running water, and agitate it with your
fingers until the pile disintegrates.

7   Let the fabric dry. Press, placing the pile side down on top of the
Velva board.

Devoré Reverse Appliqué

SUPPLIES

File folder for template

Chalk or water-soluble
    marker

Linen, cotton, or rayon
    base fabric

Silk or polyester appliqué
    fabric

Tear-away stabilizer

Embroidery foot

Polyester thread

Small nylon-bristle brush

Fiber-Etch

Press cloth

1   Prewash all the fabrics. Prepare a paper template of the design.

2   Using chalk or a water-soluble marker, trace the design onto right side of the base fabric (linen, rayon, or cotton).

3   Cut a piece of appliqué fabric (silk or polyester) and a piece of tear-away stabilizer; each should be larger than the design.

4   With the right side up, center the appliqué fabric and then the stabilizer under the design area of the base fabric. Pin the layers together.

5   Place the embroidery foot in the sewing machine. Use polyester thread in both the needle and the bobbin. Use only 100% polyester thread, because the Fiber-Etch will eat cotton and rayon threads.

6 Set the machine for a 2-mm- to 3-mm-wide satin stitch.

7 Stitch along the design lines through all the layers.

8 Remove the stabilizer.

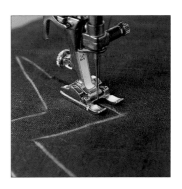

9 Use the squeeze bottle or a small brush to apply a medium coat of Fiber-Etch inside the design area.

10 Preheat a dry iron to the wool setting.

11 Place the press cloth over the design area, and press until the Fiber-Etch turns light brown and becomes brittle.

12 Rinse the fabric under running water, and agitate the base layer with your fingers until the design area disintegrates.

13 Let the fabric dry. Remove the extra appliqué fabric, and press.

Embossing

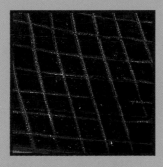

EMBOSSING IS A TECHNIQUE FOR IMPRINTING A DESIGN or texture into a pile fabric, such as velvet or velveteen. Flat areas are "carved" into the pile surface of a fabric by using a resist and a dry iron. Simple rubber stamps, small metal objects, and textured fabrics make interesting carving tools. Experiment with a variety of materials to create new effects. Rayon-blend velvets reveal the most visible impressions. Always test fabrics before beginning your project to make sure they retain an impression. Place a single embossed design on a shirt pocket or use multiple motifs to embellish a scarf or vest. Fabrics should not be washed; if laundering is necessary, dry-clean so the embossed surface is retained.

Embossing Velvet
with a Rubber Stamp

EASY

SUPPLIES

RAYON-BLEND VELVET

RUBBER FABRIC STAMP

SPRAY BOTTLE FILLED
 WITH WATER

1   Cut a piece of velvet to the desired finished size.

2   Preheat the iron to a medium-high temperature.

3   Place the rubber stamp right side up on the ironing board.

4   Place the velvet pile side down on top of the stamp.

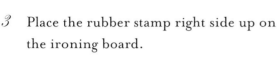
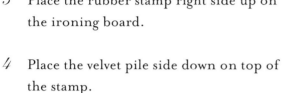

5   Spritz the back of the velvet with water.

6   Press the iron firmly over the stamp for approximately 20 seconds. Move the iron as little as possible.

7   Lift the iron and velvet from the stamp.

8   Reposition the velvet and repeat the embossing as desired.

❖ IF THE STEAM HOLES OF THE IRON leave an impression, reposition the iron or gently move it over the stamp after the first five seconds of heating.

❖ TO ADD COLOR to the embossed areas, apply fabric paint to the rubber stamp before pressing.

Embossing Velvet
with a Wire Rack

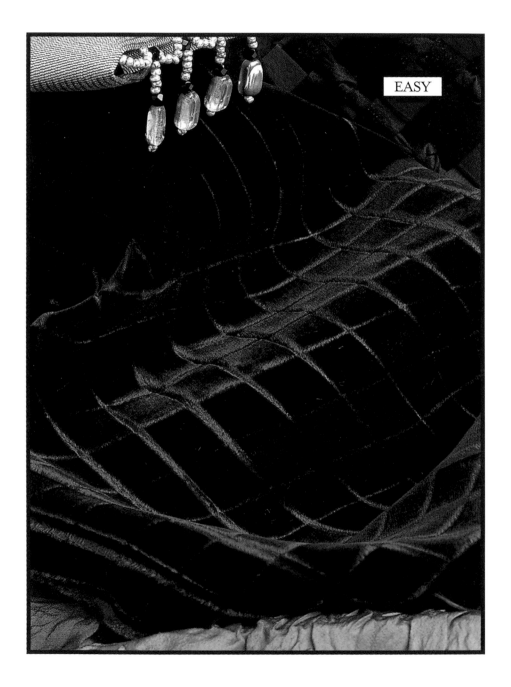

EASY

1. Cut a piece of velvet to the desired finished size.

2. Preheat the iron to a medium-high temperature.

SUPPLIES

RAYON-BLEND VELVET

WIRE COOLING RACK

SPRAY BOTTLE FILLED WITH WATER

3. Place the wire rack right side up on the ironing board.

4. Place the velvet pile side down on top of the rack.

5. Spritz the back of the velvet with water.

6. Press the iron firmly over rack for approximately 20 seconds. Reposition the iron as needed over the rack.

7. Lift the iron and velvet from the rack.

8. Reposition the velvet and repeat the embossing as desired.

❖ EXPERIMENT WITH OTHER embossing materials, such as metal mesh, wire paper clips, and heavy lace.

CHAPTER 9

Fagoting

FAGOTING USES A DECORATIVE STITCH TO CREATE AN open joining between sections of fabric. A technique once done only by hand, it can now be duplicated with machine embroidery stitches. Traditional hand fagoting is given a new twist with the use of beads. Lightweight to medium-weight crisp fabrics, such as linen and cotton, are recommended. Stitch with cotton and rayon threads; the thread can be doubled for added definition. Any decorative stitch with a minimum width of 4 mm can be used with this technique. Make samples of the stitches first, because stitches often look much different over an open space. The edges of the fabrics must be folded or otherwise finished before joining them with fagoting. Use fagoting to add details to pockets, hems, and home decorating projects at nonstress areas.

Machine Fagoting

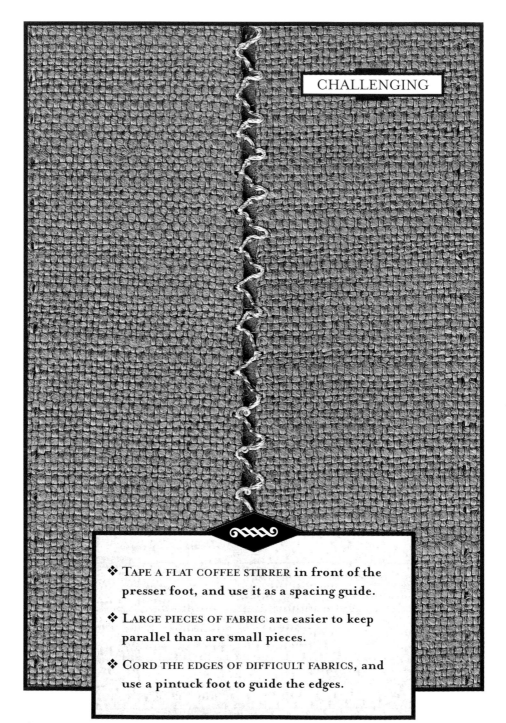

CHALLENGING

❖ TAPE A FLAT COFFEE STIRRER in front of the
   presser foot, and use it as a spacing guide.

❖ LARGE PIECES OF FABRIC are easier to keep
   parallel than are small pieces.

❖ CORD THE EDGES OF DIFFICULT FABRICS, and
   use a pintuck foot to guide the edges.

1 Prewash all fabrics.

SUPPLIES

SPRAY STABILIZER
EMBROIDERY FOOT
EMBROIDERY THREAD

2 Fold or finish the edges of the
fabrics to be fagoted.

3 Apply a coat of spray stabilizer
to the folded or finished edges of the fabric. Press with a dry iron.

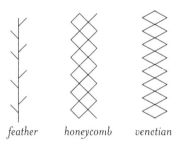

feather   *honeycomb*   *venetian*

4 Place the embroidery foot in the
sewing machine. Set the machine
for a 5-mm-wide decorative
stitch, such as feather, zigzag,
honeycomb, or venetian hemstitch. Thread the needle with two
strands of embroidery thread, and
fill the bobbin with embroidery thread. For the sample shown here,
I used a 5-mm-wide by 2.5-mm-long feather stitch. The tension
was set at 3.5.

5 Place the folded edges of the fabric under the embroidery foot so
that they are facing each other and are spaced about ⅛ in. apart.

6 Begin stitching. Adjust the space
between the fabrics as necessary. The
stitch should catch one folded edge,
cross the open space, and then catch
the parallel folded edge. Stitch slowly
and evenly.

7 Continue stitching until complete. Remove the spray starch.

Hand-Beaded Fagoting

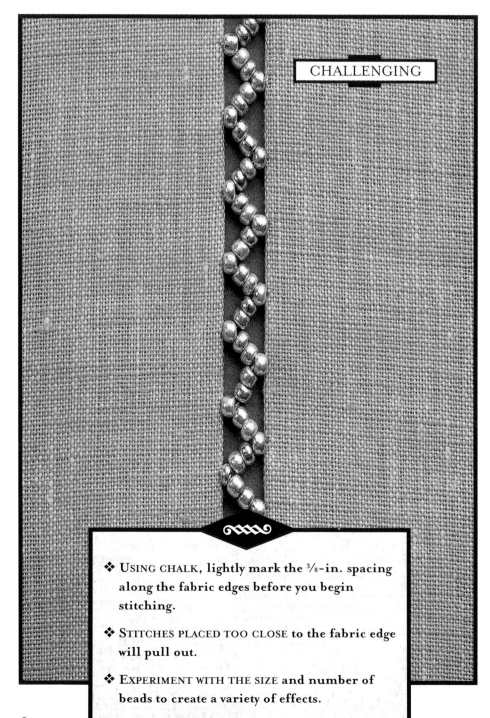

❖ USING CHALK, lightly mark the ³⁄₈-in. spacing along the fabric edges before you begin stitching.

❖ STITCHES PLACED TOO CLOSE to the fabric edge will pull out.

❖ EXPERIMENT WITH THE SIZE and number of beads to create a variety of effects.

1 Fold or finish the edges of the fabrics to be fagoted.

SUPPLIES

BEADING NEEDLE
SILK OR WAXED COTTON THREAD
SEED BEADS

2 Thread the beading needle with silk or waxed cotton thread. Knot the end of the thread.

3 Bury the knot in one fabric edge.

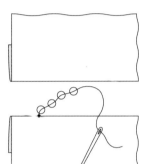

4 Make a small knot and pull the thread taut. String on four seed beads.

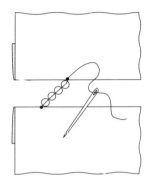

5 Take a small stitch in the other finished edge of fabric. Pull taut and knot.

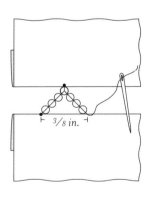

6 Insert the needle through the closest bead. String on three seed beads. Cross back to the other finished edge, and take a small stitch approximately ³/₈ in. away from the original knot.

7 Continue beading and knotting for the first three anchor stitches. Then knot every 2 in. as the beading progresses. Maintain the ³/₈-in. space between the anchor stitches. At the end of the fagoting join, knot the last three anchor stitches.

10

Fringing

FRINGE IS A DECORATIVE LOOSE OR FRAYED EDGING that can be applied to garments, home decorating projects, and crafts projects. Embellish seams and hems with fringe accents. Fringed fabric can be created by removing threads from an unfinished edge. The sewing machine's tailor tack foot is a useful tool for constructing short, dense thread fringe. Loops are formed over the center bar of the foot and secured with a decorative stitch. Fringe can also be created out of threads, cords, and ribbons, which are couched onto the surface of the base fabric. The length of the fringe is determined by the weight of the fabric and the end use of the project.

Self-Fringed Fabric Edge

EASY

1 Determine the desired finished length of the fringe. (Heavier, coarser woven fabric can accommodate a wider fringed edge.)

2 Cut the fabric, allowing for the fringe width.

3 Set the sewing machine for a short, narrow zigzag stitch.

4 Stitch inside the raw edge of the fabric at the top of the fringe area. (If the fringe width is to be ³/₄ in., stitch ³/₄ in. inside the raw edge.)

5 Gently remove the cross threads from the fringed edge.

❖ It is best to cut the fringe **on the lengthwise grain.**

❖ To speed removal of the threads, **clip the fabric perpendicular to the stitching line every few inches.**

❖ Fringed piping can be cut **from the selvage edge of the fabric.**

Couched Thread or Ribbon Fringe

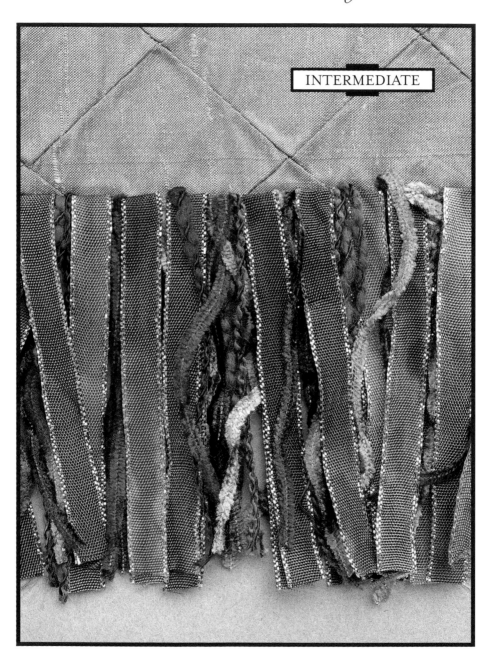

INTERMEDIATE

1 Finish the edge of the base fabric.

SUPPLIES

DECORATIVE THREADS, CORDS, OR RIBBONS

REMOVABLE TRANSPARENT TAPE

2 Determine the desired finished length of the fringe.

3 Cut the threads, cord, or ribbons to twice the desired finished length of the fringe.

4 Cut 5-in.- to 6-in.-long pieces of transparent tape.

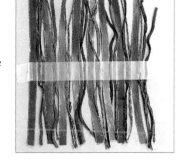

5 Line up the cut pieces of thread in a single-layer, straight row. Place the tape down the center of the row, as shown.

6 Repeat the process until enough fringe is created.

7 With right side of the fabric facing up, place the fringe with the tape strips sticky side down along the finished edge of the fabric.

8 Set the sewing machine for a short straight stitch. Stitch through the center of the tape, inside the finished edge. Add additional strips of fringe to complete the project.

9 Gently remove the transparent tape.

10 Arrange the fringe so both ends fall away from the fabric. Press and trim as necessary.

Fringing with a Tailor Tack Foot

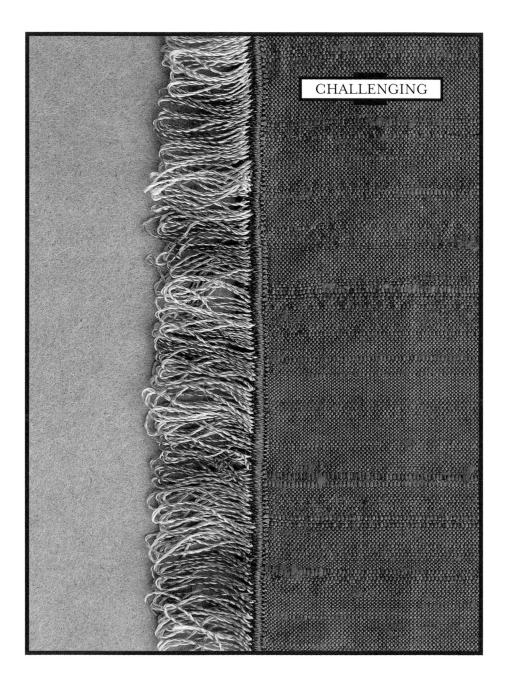

CHALLENGING

1 Press the seam or hem allowance of the base fabric to the wrong side.

SUPPLIES

Scrap fabric
Tailor tack foot
Decorative thread
Bobbinfil
Embroidery foot

2 Cut a piece of scrap fabric the length of the pressed edge.

3 Place the tailor tack foot in the sewing machine. Set the machine to a 2-mm- to 4-mm-wide satin stitch. Thread the needle with a decorative thread, and use Bobbinfil in the bobbin. Tighten the needle tension setting.

4 With right sides up, align the pressed edge of the base fabric and the raw edge of the scrap fabric. Center the fabrics under the tailor tack foot.

5 Stitch. The needle should move through the base fabric on one side of the foot and the scrap fabric on the other side.

6 When the stitching is complete, carefully remove the stitching from the stitch finger of the tailor tack foot. With the wrong side of the fabric up, gently pull the bobbin thread from the stitching. The fabrics will separate and be joined by only the upper threads.

7 Place the embroidery foot in the machine. Set the machine to a 2-mm- to 3-mm-wide satin stitch. Adjust the needle tension setting to normal.

8 Place the base fabric under the presser foot. Stitch over the top edge of the fringe, securing it to the fabric.

9 Remove the scrap fabric from the bottom of the fringe. The excess seam allowance can be trimmed from the wrong side of the pressed edge if desired.

❖ EXPERIMENT WITH VARIEGATED THREAD for the fringe or for a decorative securing stitch.

❖ PLACE TEAR-AWAY STABILIZER under the fabric when anchoring the fringe with a decorative stitch.

11

Hemstitching

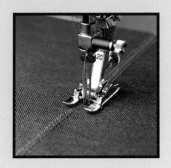

WIDELY USED IN HEIRLOOM SEWING, HEMSTITCHING IS a technique that creates delicate lacelike holes in fabric. Wing needles separate the fabric threads, and stitching pulls and secures the holes in place. Two types of needles are used to create machine hemstitching: single-wing needles, which vary in size from 90/14 to 120/20, and double-wing needles, which are made up of one size 100/16 wing needle and one size 80/12 universal needle. Single-wing needles are used for sewing adjoining rows of zigzag stitching or decorative built-in hemstitches. Double-wing needles have a more limited application and are solely used to sew adjoining rows of straight stitching. Crisp, lightweight natural fabrics—such as linen, cotton, organdy, and organza—produce the most attractive results with these techniques.

Single-Wing Needle: Zigzag Adjoining Rows

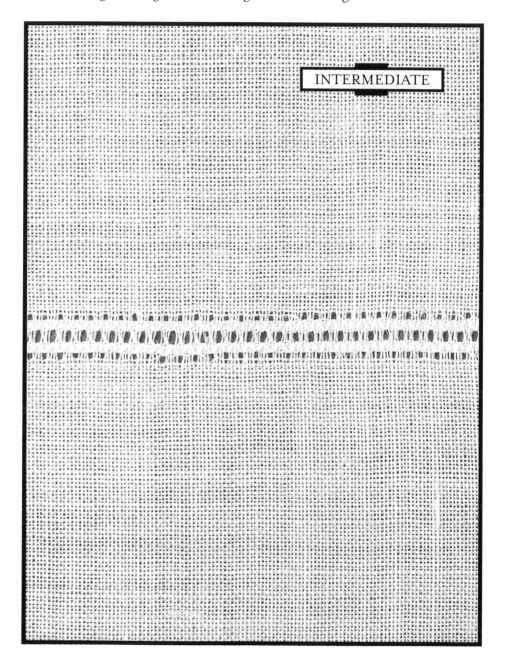

INTERMEDIATE

SUPPLIES

SPRAY-ON STABILIZER

CHALK OR WATER-SOLUBLE
   MARKER

OPEN-TOE EMBROIDERY FOOT

100/16 SINGLE-WING NEEDLE

COTTON OR RAYON
   EMBROIDERY THREAD

BOBBINFIL

TEAR-AWAY STABILIZER
   (OPTIONAL)

1   Prewash the fabric.

2   Apply a coat of spray-on stabilizer to the fabric. Press with a dry iron. Repeat, adding layers of spray-on stabilizer until the fabric is fairly stiff.

3   Mark the stitching line on the fabric with chalk or a water-soluble marker.

4   Place the open-toe embroidery foot and wing needle in the sewing machine. Thread the needle with embroidery thread, and use Bobbin-fil in the bobbin. Set the machine for a 1.75-mm- to 2-mm-wide by 1-mm-long zigzag stitch. (A layer of tear-away stabilizer can be placed under the fabric for additional strength.) Stitch a row of zigzag

stitches. At the end of the row, stop stitching with the needle down on the left swing.

5 Raise the embroidery foot, and turn the fabric so the needle is now at the top of the stitching.

6 Lower the foot, and slowly stitch a second row of zigzag stitches.

7 The left swing of the needle should land exactly in the right holes of the previous stitching.

8 Continue stitching rows as desired.

9 Remove the tear-away stabilizer, if used. Remove the spray-on stabilizer by soaking the fabric in warm water.

❖ A TRIPLE ZIGZAG STITCH produces prominent stitching and holes.

❖ USE THE BALANCE ADJUSTMENT to correct the stitch alignment.

❖ AN EVEN, MODERATE STITCH SPEED can be maintained with the half speed setting.

❖ STITCHING ON THE BIAS OR CROSSWISE GRAIN produces more defined holes than does stitching on the lengthwise grain.

Single-Wing Needle: Decorative Stitch

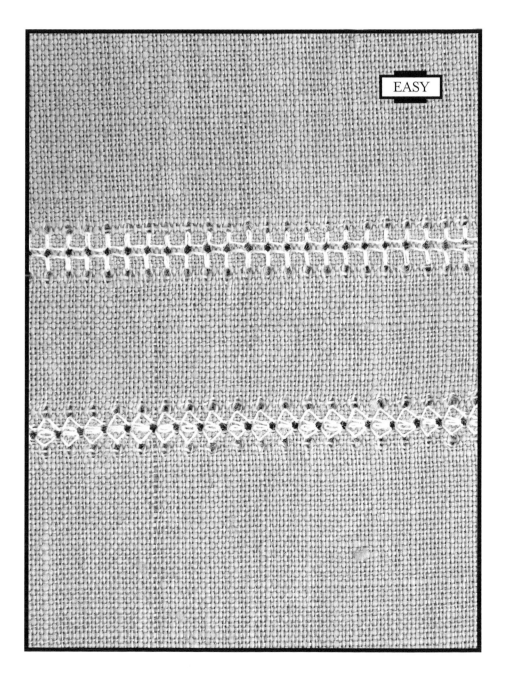

EASY

SUPPLIES

SPRAY-ON STABILIZER

CHALK OR WATER-SOLUBLE
   MARKER

OPEN-TOE EMBROIDERY FOOT

100/16 SINGLE-WING NEEDLE

COTTON OR RAYON EMBROI-
   DERY THREAD

BOBBINFIL

TEAR-AWAY STABILIZER
   (OPTIONAL)

1   Prewash the fabric.

2   Apply a coat of spray-on stabilizer to the fabric. Press with a dry iron. Repeat, adding layers of spray-on stabilizer until the fabric is fairly stiff.

3   Mark the stitching line on the fabric with chalk or a water-soluble marker.

4   Place the open-toe embroidery foot and wing needle in the sewing machine. Thread the needle with embroidery thread, and use Bobbinfil in the bobbin. Set the machine for a built-in hemstitch—such as Parisian, which looks like an L, or venetian, which produces a diamond pattern. Use a 2-mm-wide by 2-mm- to 2.5-mm-long Parisian stitch or a 3.5-mm-wide by 3-mm-long venetian stitch. (A layer of tear-away stabilizer can be placed under the fabric for additional strength.)

Parisian   *venetian*

5   Stitch as desired.

6   Remove the tear-away stabilizer, if used. Remove the spray-on stabilizer by soaking the fabric in warm water.

Double-Wing Needle: Straight Stitch

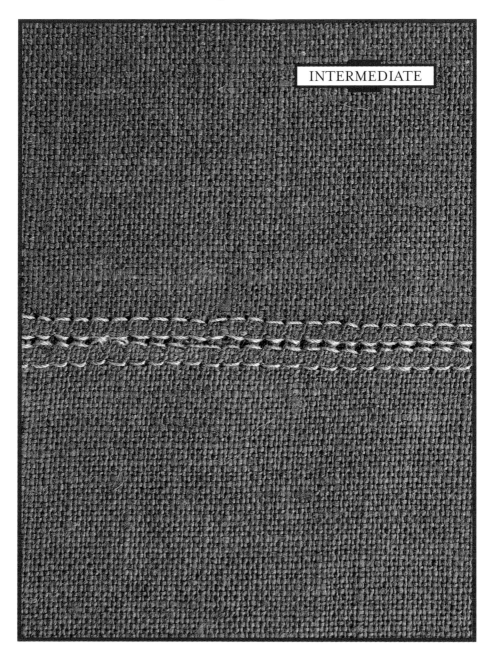

INTERMEDIATE

SUPPLIES

SPRAY-ON STABILIZER

CHALK OR WATER-SOLUBLE

   MARKER

OPEN-TOE EMBROIDERY FOOT

100/16 DOUBLE-WING NEEDLE

COTTON OR RAYON EMBROI-

   DERY THREAD (2 SPOOLS)

BOBBINFIL

TEAR-AWAY STABILIZER

   (OPTIONAL)

1 Prewash the fabric.

2 Apply a medium coat of spray-on stabilizer to the fabric. Press with a dry iron. Repeat, adding layers of spray-on stabilizer until the fabric is fairly stiff.

3 Mark the stitching line on the fabric with chalk or a water-soluble marker.

4 Place the open-toe embroidery foot and wing needle in the sewing machine. Thread the needles with embroidery thread, and use Bobbinfil in the bobbin. Set the machine for a 2-mm- to 2.5-mm-long straight stitch. (A layer of tear-away stabilizer can be placed under the fabric for additional strength.)

5 Stitch the row to the desired length.

6 Turn the fabric so that the end of the stitching is now at the beginning. Lower the wing needle into the last hole made in the previous stitching. Slowly stitch the second row, keeping the wing needle aligned with the previous holes. Lightly pull the fabric to the front or back when adjustments are needed.

7 Continue stitching rows as desired.

8 Remove the tear-away stabilizer, if used. Remove the spray-on stabilizer by soaking the fabric in warm water.

SINGLE-WING NEEDLE

❖ EXPERIMENT WITH OTHER DECORATIVE STITCHES, such as the Turkish stitch, honeycomb stitch, ladder stitch, and picot stitch.

| *Turkish* | *honeycomb* | *ladder* | *picot* |

DOUBLE-WING NEEDLE

❖ USE THIS TECHNIQUE as decorative topstitching on hems.

CHAPTER 12

Laminating

LAMINATING IS A PROCESS OF BONDING TWO FLAT surfaces together with an adhesive. Layers of fabric can be adhered to one another with fusible web or with fabric glue. Fusible web is a heat-activated glue that is bonded to a paper backing. There are many different brands available; some create a denser bond than do others. Experiment to see which type works best for each project. Fabric glue may be applied to the base fabric with a brush, stamp, or stencil for a variety of design possibilities. Nonwoven materials, such as metallic foil, can be joined to fabric with either method. Office-supply, craft, hobby, and chain fabric stores are good sources for metallic foil. For best results, always refer to the manufacturer's instructions.

Laminating
Fabric to Fabric

EASY

SUPPLIES

FILE FOLDER FOR TEMPLATE
(OPTIONAL)
NO. 2 PENCIL (OPTIONAL)
LIGHTWEIGHT FUSIBLE WEB
PRESS CLOTHS

1 Prepare a paper template of the design, if you'd like.

2 Cut a piece of fusible web slightly larger than the design.

3 Press the nonpaper side of the fusible web to the wrong side of the design fabric, following the manufacturer's instructions.

4 If you're using one, place the template wrong side up on the paper backing of the fusible web. Using a no. 2 pencil, trace the design onto the paper.

5 Cut out the design.

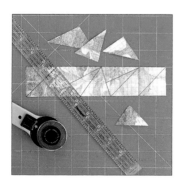

6 Remove the paper backing from the fusible web. Place the base fabric on the ironing board. Place a press cloth underneath the fabric. Position the design pieces right side up on the right side of the base fabric.

7 Place another press cloth on top of the design pieces. Fuse the design in place, following the manufacturer's instructions.

8 Continue cutting and fusing as desired.

VARIATION

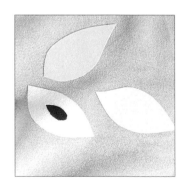

◆ Cut shapes out of the center of the laminated motif after fusing it in place. The cut edges will not fray.

Laminating Metallic Foil to Fabric

EASY

SUPPLIES

FABRIC GLUE OR GLUE RECOM-
MENDED FOR METALLIC FOIL
SHALLOW CONTAINER

BRUSH OR STAMP
IRON-ON METALLIC FOIL
PRESS CLOTH

1 With the right side up, lay out the fabric on a flat, firm surface.

2 Pour a small amount of fabric glue into a shallow container.

3 Brush or stamp the glue onto the fabric.

4 Let the glue dry completely. Clean the brush with soap and water.

5 Heat a dry iron to the cotton setting. Place the fabric on the ironing board.

6 Cut pieces of iron-on foil large enough to cover the design area.

7 With the foil side facing up, place the foil over the dried glue areas.

8 Place a press cloth on top of the foil. Press to fuse the foil, following the manufacturer's instructions. (The time varies by brand of foil. Test before fusing to your finished project.)

9 Remove the press cloth. Peel the clear cellophane coating off the top of the foil. (Some brands of foil give better results if they're completely cool before peeling; others can be removed when still warm. Experiment.)

10 Repeat these steps as desired.

VARIATION

◆ For lines and squiggle designs, squeeze the glue directly out of the bottle onto the fabric.

❖ IF THE FOIL DOES NOT COMPLETELY COVER THE GLUE AREAS, **place a second piece of foil over the glue, and press.**

❖ EXPERIMENT WITH APPLYING THE GLUE WITH STAMPS **and with using stencils.**

❖ LAYERS OF FOIL CAN BE APPLIED **on top of one another to create interesting textural effects.**

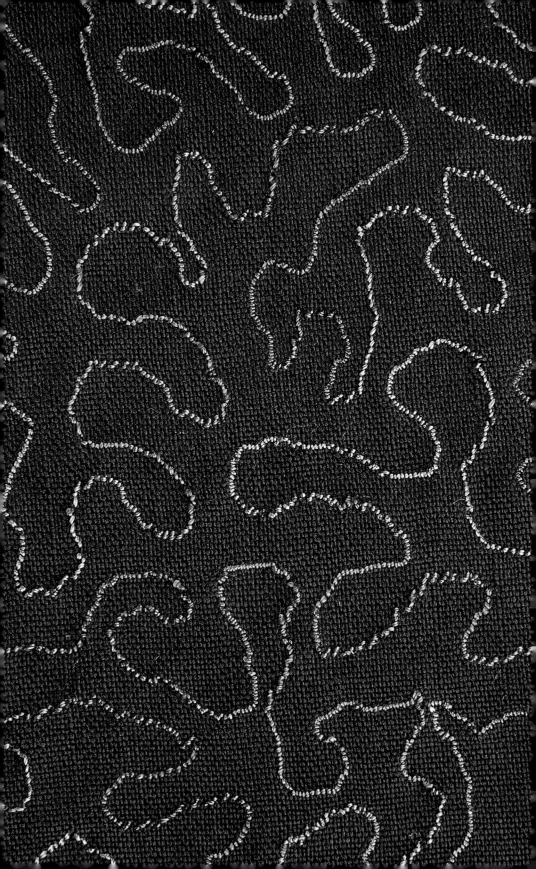

CHAPTER

Machine Embroidery

MACHINE EMBROIDERY REFERS TO A BROAD RANGE of embellishment techniques. Most stitches fall into one of two categories: standard utility or decorative machine-stitch patterns, which are produced with a presser foot, and free-motion embroidery stitches, which are done with a darning foot or no presser foot at all and with the sewing machine feed dogs lowered. The best results with these techniques are achieved with an embroidery needle and embroidery thread. Heavier threads are appropriate with heavier fabrics and when used in the bobbin. Cotton and rayon embroidery threads are available in a range of colors. Free-motion work requires practice and patience at first, but the creative possibilities are endless.

Decorative Stitch Patterns: Lines

EASY

SUPPLIES

STABILIZER

CHALK MARKER (OPTIONAL)

EMBROIDERY FOOT

EMBROIDERY NEEDLE

DECORATIVE EMBROIDERY
THREAD

BOBBINFIL

1   Prewash the fabric.

2   Select an appropriate stabilizer for the
fabric. (Use spray-on or water-soluble
stabilizer on delicate fabrics, heat or
tear-away stabilizer on medium to heavy
fabrics.) Make a sample before beginning your project.

3   Using a chalk marker, draw the design onto the right side of fabric,
if you'd like.

4   Place the embroidery foot and needle in the sewing machine.
Thread the needle with embroidery thread, and use Bobbinfil in
the bobbin. Select the desired utility or decorative stitch.

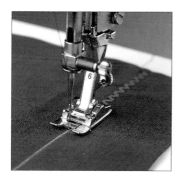

5   Stitch the design, following the chalk
lines, if used.

6   Remove any extra stabilizer by following the manufacturer's instructions.
Press.

❖ ADJUST THE WIDTH AND LENGTH to modify the appearance of a preprogrammed stitch.

❖ VARIEGATED THREAD produces interesting color gradations with no extra effort.

❖ USE THE MIRROR IMAGE CONTROL to reverse the left and right edges of a stitch.

VARIATION

◆ Use simple utility or decorative stitches to build a motif.

Free-Motion: Straight Stitch

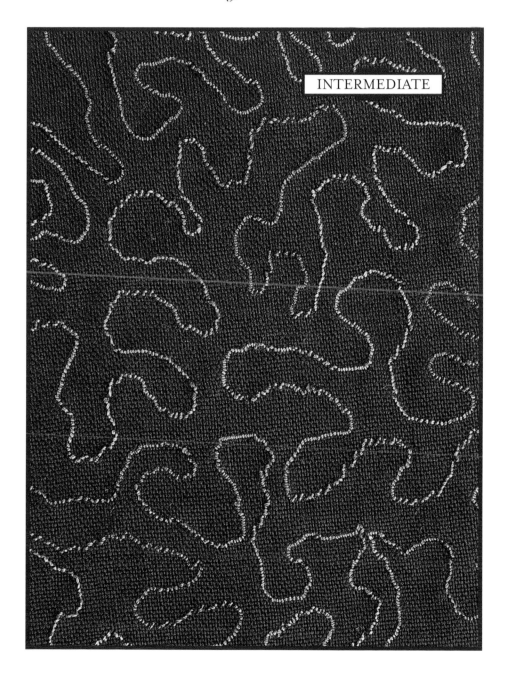

INTERMEDIATE

1   Prewash the fabric.

SUPPLIES

CHALK MARKER (OPTIONAL)
EMBROIDERY HOOP
OPEN MACHINE-EMBROIDERY
  OR DARNING FOOT
EMBROIDERY THREAD
BOBBINFIL

2   If desired, use a chalk marker to draw the design onto the right side of the fabric.

3   Stretch the fabric into an embroidery hoop. With right side up, lay the fabric on top of the outer ring of the hoop; then insert the inner ring and tighten the screw. The fabric should be tight in the hoop, like a drum.

4   Lower the feed dogs of the sewing machine or cover them with tape.

5   Place the open machine-embroidery or darning foot in the machine. (This technique may also be done with no foot in the machine.) Place an embroidery needle in the machine and thread it with embroidery thread. Place Bobbinfil in the bobbin.

6   Set the machine to a straight length of 0 mm. Place the hooped fabric right side up under the embroidery foot. Lower the presser foot lever. Bring up the bobbin thread, and stitch two to three small locking stitches. Clip the threads.

7   Begin stitching. (The thread tension may need to be loosened. You will need to readjust for each type of thread and fabric used.)

8 Complete the stitching using a freehand technique, following the chalk lines if used. The photo on page 99 shows a freehand meandering stitch.

❖ OPTIMUM CONTROL IS ACHIEVED by running the machine fast and guiding the hoop slowly.

❖ OVERLAP AND BUILD UP STITCHES to form texture and color gradations.

❖ EXPERIMENT WITH A VARIETY of specialty metallic, variegated, and rayon threads.

VARIATIONS

◆ Zigzag filler stitch: set the machine for a 1-mm- to 5-mm-wide zigzag stitch.

◆ French knot stitch: Set the machine for a 4-mm-wide zigzag stitch. Stitch several times to form a knot. Move the work, and stitch again. Single floating threads connect the knots.

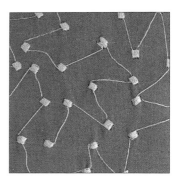

Free-Motion:
Cable Stitch

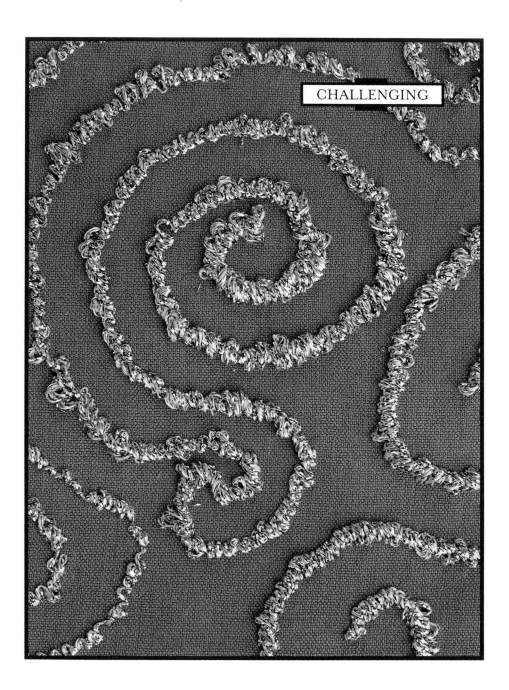

CHALLENGING

SUPPLIES

FUSIBLE INTERFACING
(OPTIONAL)
CHALK MARKER (OPTIONAL)
EMBROIDERY HOOP
WATER-SOLUBLE STABILIZER
(OPTIONAL)
HEAVY DECORATIVE THREAD

EXTRA BOBBIN CASE
COTTON EMBROIDERY OR
POLYESTER THREAD
OPEN MACHINE-EMBROIDERY
OR DARNING FOOT
EMBROIDERY THREAD

1 Prewash the fabric.

2 Fuse the interfacing to the wrong side of the fabric in the design area, if desired.

3 If you'd like, trace the design onto the wrong side of the fabric using a chalk marker.

4 Stretch the fabric into an embroidery hoop. With the wrong side up,
lay the fabric on top of the outer
hoop; then insert the inner ring,
and tighten the screw. The fabric
should be tight in the hoop, like a
drum. Add a layer of water-soluble
stabilizer on top of the fabric if,
needed.

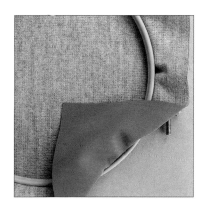

5 Lower the feed dogs of the sewing machine or cover them with tape.

6 Wind a heavy decorative thread onto the bobbin. This can be accomplished by hand winding or on the machine, by leaving the thread out of the tension stud and winding at slow speed.

7 Insert the bobbin into an extra bobbin case, and loosen the tension until the thread pulls freely from the case. Thread the needle with cotton embroidery or polyester thread, and tighten the needle tension.

8 Place an open machine-embroidery or darning foot in the machine. (This technique may also be done with no foot in the machine.)

9 Place the hooped fabric wrong side up under the embroidery foot. Lower the presser foot lever. Bring up the bobbin thread, and stitch two to three small locking stitches. Clip the threads. Set the machine for a 0-mm-long by 1.5-mm-wide zigzag stitch. Begin stitching with a free-hand technique, following the chalk lines, if used.

10 Continue stitching as desired. Remove any extra stabilizer by following the manufacturer's instructions.

❖ ADJUST THE BOBBIN TENSION to control the amount of looping on the right side of the fabric. Looser tension produces more height; tighter tension produces a flatter, couched effect.

❖ IF THE HOOP IS GUIDED TOO SLOWLY, the stitches will pile up and break; if the hoop is guided too quickly, the stitches will lose the bouclé effect.

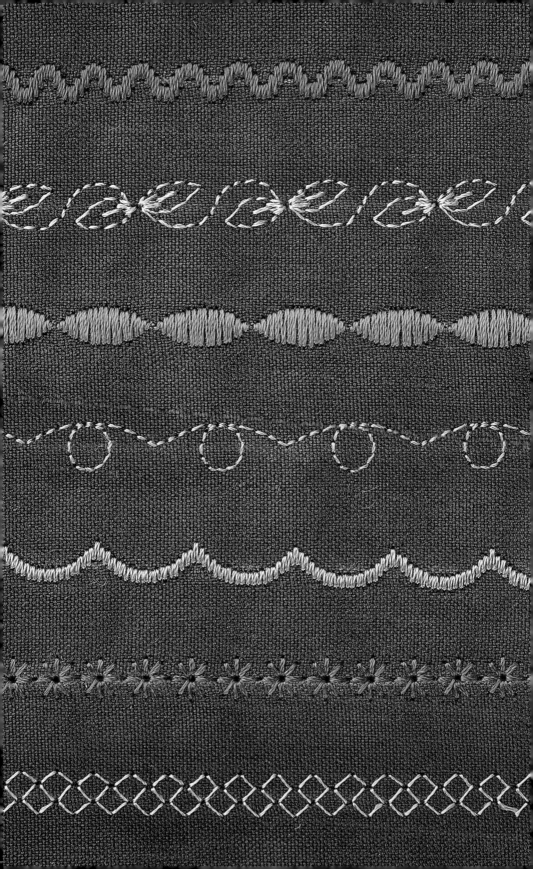

CHAPTER 14

Piping

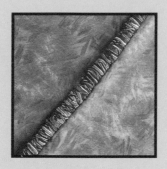

PIPING IS AN INSERTED DECORATIVE SEAM OR EDGE FINISH. Flat or corded, large or small, piping can be constructed out of a variety of materials, such as fabric, leather, suede, ribbon, lace, fringe, and purchased trims. Piping is frequently used as an accent on garment pockets and cuffs and on home decorating projects. Cord covered with bias-cut fabric is most commonly used and referred to as piping. Rattail cord provides the perfect smooth, firm filling for small covered piping. The standard sewing-machine accessory used to make piping is the zipper foot; but many machine brands now have specialized feet available, such as the piping foot, cording foot, and pin-tuck foot, to make the execution of this technique more precise.

Basic Flat Piping

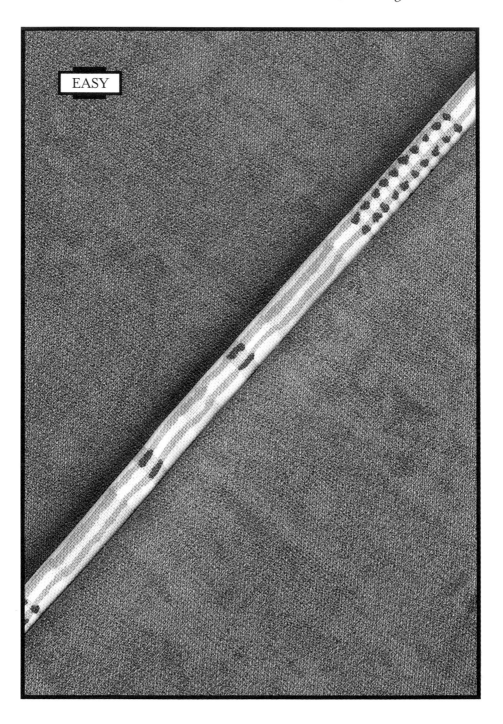

EASY

1   Determine the finished width and length of the piping. (It never hurts to have extra.)

SUPPLIES

RULER

2   Cut fabric strips twice the finished width plus two seam allowances. Cut the strips on the bias for curved and angled seams and hems. If the piping is to be inserted in a straight seam or hem, the fabric may be cut on the lengthwise or crosswise grain. Cut leather, suede, and knits on the crosswise grain.

3   Join the ends of the fabric strips to form the needed length of piping.

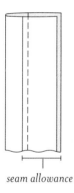

seam allowance

4   With wrong sides together, fold the fabric strip in half lengthwise. Stitch the raw edges together slightly to the right of the seamline.

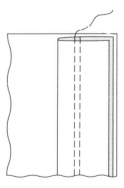

5   With the right side of the base fabric up, align the raw edges of the piping and fabric. Pin in place. Stitch, using the previous stitching as a guide.

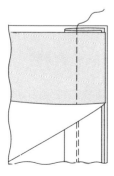

6   With right sides together, place the remaining base fabric over the piping, aligning the raw edges. The piping should be sandwiched between the fabric layers. Pin in place. Stitch along the seamline. Press.

Basic Corded Piping

INTERMEDIATE

1 Determine the finished width and length of the piping. (It never hurts to have extra.)

SUPPLIES

RATTAIL OR COTTON CABLE
    CORD
RULER
ZIPPER FOOT, CORDING
    FOOT, OR PINTUCK FOOT

2 Wrap a piece of the piping fabric around the cord, and pin close to the cord. Remove the cord, and measure the fabric. Cut the fabric strips; their width should equal the width around the cord plus two seam allowances. Cut the strips on the bias for curved and angled seams and hems. If

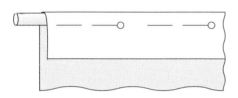

the piping is to be inserted in a straight seam or hem, the fabric may be cut on the lengthwise or crosswise grain. Cut leather, suede, and knits on the crosswise grain.

3 Join the ends of the fabric strips to form the needed length of piping.

4 With wrong sides together, wrap the fabric strip around the cord. Align the raw edges, and pin.

5 Place the zipper, cording, or pintuck foot in the sewing machine. Set the needle to the half left position for the zipper foot or to the far right position for the cording or pintuck foot. Stitch, guiding the cording along the left edge of the zipper foot or through the center groove of the cording or pintuck foot.

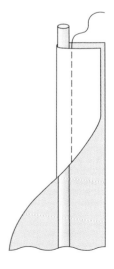

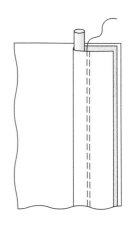

6   With the right side of the base fabric up, align the raw edges of the piping and fabric. Pin in place. Stitch, using the previous stitching as a guide.

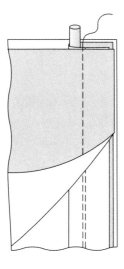

7   With right sides together, place the remaining base fabric over the piping, and align the raw edges. The piping should be sandwiched between the fabric layers. Turn the work over, and pin in place. Set the needle to the far left position for the zipper foot or the half right position for the cording or pintuck foot. Stitch along the seamline. The stitching should fall to the left of the first line of stitches. Press.

❖ IT IS IMPORTANT THAT THE FINAL ROW of stitches be closest to the cording. This ensures that no previous stitching will show on the right side.

❖ THE CORDING MAY BE REMOVED from the piping after the final stitching to reduce stiffness.

❖ CLIP THE PIPING almost to the stitching around curves and at the pivot points of corners for a smooth finished appearance.

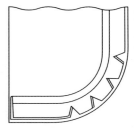

Shirred Piping

INTERMEDIATE

1 Determine the finished
width and length of the
piping. (It never hurts to
have extra.)

SUPPLIES

RULER

LEATHER-ROLLER FOOT OR
ZIPPER FOOT

CORD

2 Wrap a piece of the piping fabric around the cord, and pin close to
the cord. Remove the cord, and measure the fabric. Cut the fabric
strips; their width should equal the width around the cord plus two
seam allowances. Cut the strips on the bias for curved and angled

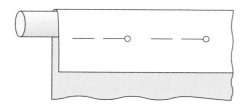

seams and hems. If the piping is
to be inserted in a straight seam
or hem, the fabric may be cut on
lengthwise or crosswise grain.
Cut leather, suede, and knits on
the crosswise grain.

3 Join the ends of the fabric strips to form at least twice the needed
length of piping.

4 With wrong sides together, wrap the fabric strip around the cord.
Align the raw edges, and pin.

5 Place the leather-roller or zipper foot
in the sewing machine.

6 Guide the cording along the right edge
of the foot, stitching to the left of the
seamline. Stop every few inches with the
needle down in the fabric. Shirr the
fabric behind the foot.

7   With the right side of the base fabric up, align the raw edges of the piping and fabric. Pin in place. Stitch, using the previous stitching as a guide.

8   With right sides together, place the remaining base fabric over the piping and align the raw edges. The piping should be sandwiched between the fabric layers. Turn the work over, and pin in place. Stitch along the seamline. The stitching should fall inside the first line of stitches. Press.

❖ FOR LIGHTWEIGHT FABRIC, strips can be cut up to five times longer than the finished length of the piping.

Ribbon Piping

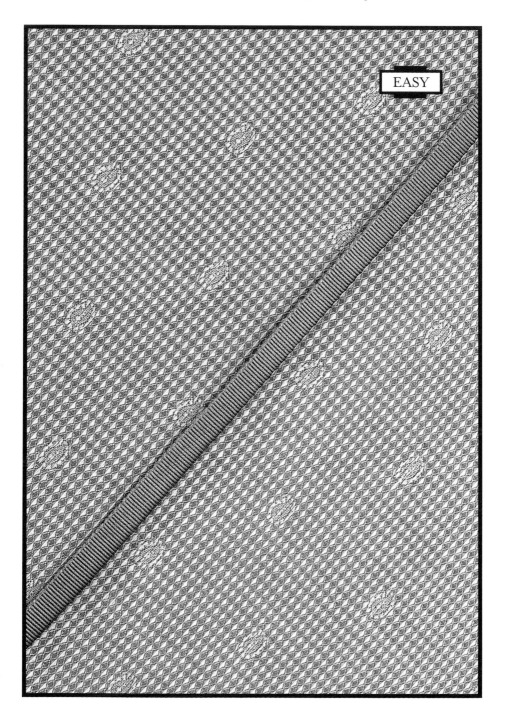

EASY

SUPPLIES

piping   seam allowance

1   Determine the finished width and length of the piping. (It never hurts to have extra.) The ribbon should be as wide as the desired finished width plus one seam allowance. Ribbon is not easily manipulated around corners or curves, unless it is bias ribbon.

2   With the right side of the base fabric up, align the edge of the ribbon with the raw edge of the base fabric. Pin in place. Stitch together slightly to the right of the seamline.

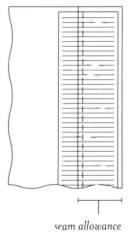

seam allowance

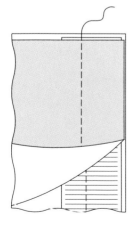

3   With right sides together, place the remaining base fabric over the ribbon and align the raw edges. The ribbon should be sandwiched between the fabric layers. Pin in place. Stitch along the seamline. Press.

15

Stamping

STAMPING IS A QUICK METHOD OF PRINTING A DESIGN,
texture, or image onto the surface of fabric. There are a
wide variety of commercial rubber stamps available for
purchase, some of which are specifically designed for use
on fabric. These stamps have less detailed designs than do
those intended for paper. Both types of stamps produce
interesting results when applied to fabric. Design possibilities are unlimited with the construction of custom
stamps, which can be made out of erasers, corks, sponges,
or household objects. The keys to getting a clear stamped
image are applying a thin coat of paint and using firm,
even pressure. After the fabric paint is heat-set with a hot
dry iron, the designs can be washed or dry-cleaned.

Using a Purchased Rubber Stamp and Fabric Paint

EASY

SUPPLIES

FABRIC PAINT

SHALLOW CONTAINER

FOAM BRUSH

RUBBER STAMP

PRESS CLOTH

1   Prewash the fabric.

2   Prepare a lightly padded work surface. This can be a tabletop padded with towels, muslin, or a pin weaving board.

3   Place the fabric right side up on the padded work surface, and pin in place around the outside edges.

4   Pour a small amount of fabric paint into a shallow container. Dip a foam brush into the paint, and apply a thin coat to the surface of the rubber stamp.

5   Firmly press the stamp onto the fabric. Slowly lift the stamp off the fabric.

6 Repeat until the design is complete. Reposition and repin the fabric as needed.

7 When you're done, clean the stamps with warm water and an old toothbrush. Let the paint cure for at least 24 hours.

8 To heat-set the cured paint, place a press cloth over the design area. Press with a hot, dry iron, following the manufacturer's instructions.

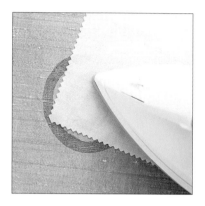

9 After heat-setting, the fabric may be machine washed or dry-cleaned.

❖ FINELY WOVEN FABRIC will allow you to produce sharp images.

❖ BLURRED IMAGES are often the result of too much paint being applied to the stamp.

❖ OVERLAP STAMPED IMAGES to create depth and texture.

Making and Using an Eraser Mosaic Stamp

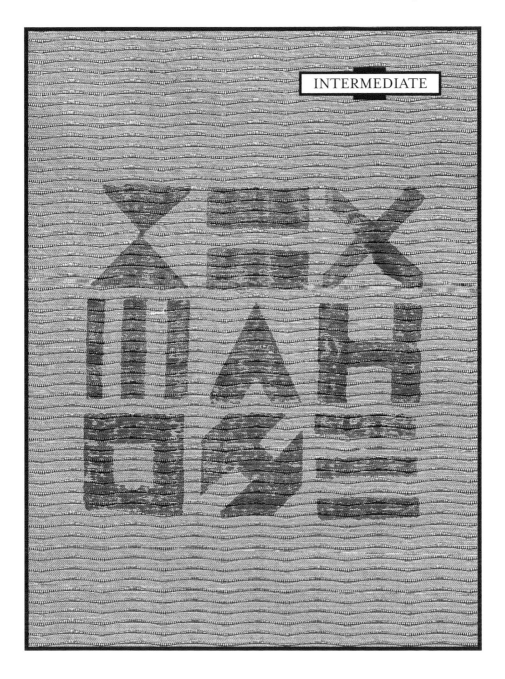

INTERMEDIATE

SUPPLIES

BALL-POINT PEN

ART-GUM ERASERS

CARDBOARD, WOOD, OR
  PLEXIGLAS

CRAFT OR UTILITY KNIFE

GLUE OR CEMENT

PRESS CLOTH

1 Using a ball-point pen, draw a simple design onto each eraser.

2 Using a craft or utility knife, cut straight down approximately ¼ in. deep into each eraser along the design lines. Carefully cut out the unwanted sections.

3 Test each design on paper, using a stamp pad. Clean the eraser stamps with water, and let dry.

4 Arrange the eraser stamps in a square or rectangular formation.

5 Cut a piece of backing material for the mosaic stamp slightly larger than the formation. The mosaic stamp can be backed with cardboard for short-term use or wood or Plexiglas for long-term use.

6 Glue the eraser stamps to the backing material, and weight with a heavy object. Let the glue dry completely.

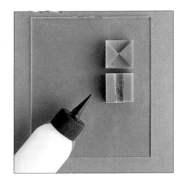

7 To complete, follow Steps 1 to 9 for "Using a Purchased Rubber Stamp and Fabric Paint."

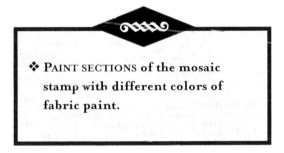

❖ PAINT SECTIONS of the mosaic stamp with different colors of fabric paint.

VARIATION

◆ A variety of thin stamp materials with adhesive backing are available in craft and hobby stores. Cut a design out of one of these materials, and adhere it to a backing for a customized stamp.

Stenciling

STENCILING IS THE SIMPLE PROCESS OF APPLYING designs to fabric through open cut-out areas of a flat sheet of cardboard or plastic. The holes cut in the stencil material make up the positive printed image. By combining and overlapping the stenciled images, you can create an almost endless array of designs. Paint, dye, or bleach can be applied using a stencil brush, foam brush, or sponge. Each type of applicator has a unique texture that will transfer to the stenciled image. Experiment to see which is most appropriate for each project. Always start with a light coat of paint, and build up the layers for more intensity. Storing stencils properly will give them a long life. Clean, dry stencils should be stored in an upright, flat position for optimum longevity.

Using a Purchased Stencil and Fabric Paint

EASY

SUPPLIES

PURCHASED STENCIL	STENCIL BRUSH OR SPONGE
FABRIC PAINT	TAPE
SHALLOW CONTAINER	PRESS CLOTH

1 Prewash the fabric.

2 Prepare a lightly padded work surface. This can be a tabletop padded with towels, muslin, or a pin weaving board.

3 Place the fabric right side up on the padded work surface, and pin in place around the outside edges.

4 Lay the stencil on top of the fabric.

5 Pour a small amount of fabric paint into a shallow container.

6 Dip a stencil brush or sponge into the paint and lightly daub up and down until the brush is evenly coated. Remove any excess paint on a piece of scrap fabric.

7 Hold the stencil securely in place with tape or your hand. Beginning in the center of the stencil, firmly apply the paint to the open areas with an up-and-down motion. Apply as many thin coats as needed to achieve the desired coverage.

8 Gently remove the stencil. Repeat until the design is complete. The paint areas should be dry before another stencil is printed on top. When finished, let the paint cure for at least 24 hours.

9 Clean the stencils after every two to three printings. Lay them flat in a sink, and gently clean with warm water. Pat them dry with paper towels and store.

10 To heat-set the cured paint, place a press cloth over the design and use a hot dry iron, following the manufacturer's instructions.

11 After heat-setting, the fabric may be machine washed or dry-cleaned.

❖ TO KEEP THE STENCIL IN PLACE, apply a light layer of spray adhesive or clear double-stick tape to the back of the stencil before placing it on top of the fabric.

❖ BLURRED IMAGES CAN RESULT FROM too much paint and/or shifting of the stencil during printing.

❖ THE SIZE OF THE BRUSH OR SPONGE is determined by the size of the stencil. Don't use a large brush with a small stencil.

❖ TO SPEED UP THE DRYING PROCESS, use a hair dryer.

❖ LAYER THE STENCIL IMAGES ON TOP of one another for depth and texture.

Making and Using a Custom Stencil

INTERMEDIATE

1   Prepare a paper template of the design. Holes cut into the stencil will be the positive printed image. Floating shapes must be joined to the main image with thin connecting bridges.

SUPPLIES

FILE FOLDER FOR TEMPLATE
CLEAR ACETATE
TAPE
SELF-HEALING CUTTING MAT
CRAFT OR UTILITY KNIFE

2   Cut a piece of acetate slightly larger than the design. Tape the template to the acetate.

3   Place the acetate on top of the self-healing cutting mat. Using a craft or utility knife, cut out the design.

4   Follow Steps I to II for "Using a Purchased Stencil and Fabric Paint."

❖ REINFORCE THE THIN connecting bridges of the stencil with strips of packing tape.

VARIATIONS

- For a shadow effect, print a second image slightly offset from the first. Use less paint to create a faint shadow.

- To create a positive image shadow, cut a solid positive image out of the stencil material. Place the stencil on the right side of the fabric. Dip the brush in the paint and dab around the outside edges of the shape to create a shadow.

- To block off sections of the stencil or fabric, use tape or paper before applying the paint.

17

Stitching
and Slashing

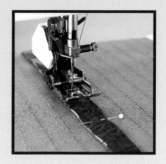

STITCHING AND SLASHING IS A TECHNIQUE FOR QUILTING several layers of fabric together and then cutting between the stitching through all but the bottom layer. Stitching designs can be simple diagonal lines, zigzags, or squares. Fabric is cut along the bias so that it will fray but not unravel excessively. The fabric sandwich is then machine washed and dried. The fabrics used must be washable and colorfast but should not be prewashed. The slashed edges of fabric "bloom" after laundering, forming a faux chenille texture. Rayon and natural fabrics, such as cotton and silk, produce the best results. Use cotton threads in the needle and bobbin. Experiment with a variety of fabric fiber, print, and texture combinations.

Stitched and Slashed Faux Chenille Fabric

INTERMEDIATE

1   Select four to seven fabrics to create the chenille. Cotton or rayon fabrics work best for the base layer.

SUPPLIES

WATER-SOLUBLE MARKER OR CHALK

WALKING FOOT

SHARP CRAFT SCISSORS

2   Make sample squares following the directions for "Making Chenille Fabric Samples" and select your favorite stacking arrangement.

3   Cut all the fabrics, adding 1 in. to the seam allowances.

4   Stack the fabrics as desired, and pin the layers together.

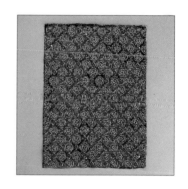

5   With the right side facing up, use a water-soluble marker or chalk to mark the top layer of the fabric with a line that is at a 45-degree angle to the straight of grain.

6   Place the walking foot in the sewing machine. Set the machine for a straight stitch, and sew along the marked line.

7 Continue stitching lines that are parallel to the first line, until the fabric is completely quilted. Allow ½ in. to ¾ in. between the stitching lines.

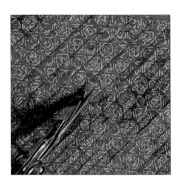

8 Using sharp craft scissors, carefully cut between the stitching lines through all but the bottom layer of fabric.

9 Recut the fabric if necessary, removing the excess seam allowance.

10 Seam, bind, or finish the raw edges of the base fabric as desired.

11 Machine wash and dry the fabric.

❖ THE STITCHING IS DONE AT A 45-DEGREE ANGLE to the straight of grain so that the fabric is slashed along the bias, allowing the fabric to crinkle but not to ravel excessively.

❖ DO NOT WASH THE FABRICS before assembling.

❖ ALTER THE DIRECTION OF THE STITCHED ROWS to create a zigzag or other geometric pattern.

❖ DO NOT USE POLYESTER OR SYNTHETIC FABRICS; they do not bloom when washed.

❖ SPECIAL SELF-HEALING CUTTING MAT STRIPS are available that can be inserted into the stitched columns. The rows can then be cut with a rotary cutter.

Making Chenille Fabric Samples

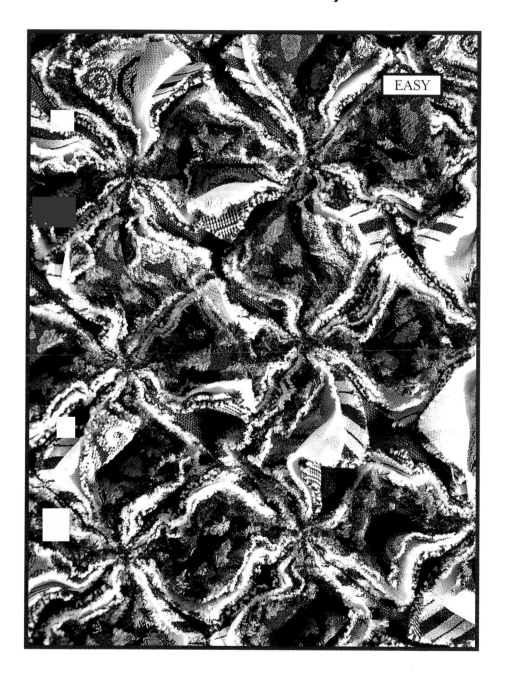

EASY

1 Select four to seven fabrics to create the chenille samples. Cut several 6-in.-square sample pieces from each fabric.

SUPPLIES

WATER-SOLUBLE MARKER OR CHALK

WALKING FOOT

SHARP CRAFT SCISSORS

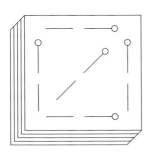

2 Form stacks of squares, changing the order of the fabrics in each stack. Pin the fabrics in each stack together.

3 With the right side facing up, use a water-soluble marker or chalk to mark a line diagonally across each stack from corner to corner.

4 Place the walking foot in the sewing machine. Set the machine for a straight stitch.

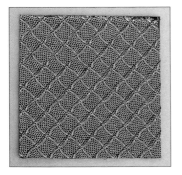

5 For each sample, sew along the marked line. Continue stitching lines that are parallel to the center line until the sample is completely quilted. Space the lines ⅝ in. apart.

6 Using sharp craft scissors, carefully cut between the stitching lines through all but the bottom layer. Cut each sample.

7 Wet the cut fabric stacks in a sink, and agitate the layers with your hands by rubbing the fabrics together. Place the samples, along with several towels, in a dryer. Set the dryer to a medium heat, and tumble until all the moisture has been removed from the samples.

8 Examine the samples and pick your preferred fabric-stacking arrangement. Follow the directions for "Stitched and Slashed Faux Chenille Fabric."

Faux Chenille Trim

INTERMEDIATE

1   Follow Steps 1 to 7 for
    "Stitched and Slashed Faux
    Chenille Fabric," except do
    not include the additional
    1 in. in the seam allowances.

SUPPLIES

SELF-HEALING CUTTING MAT
ROTARY CUTTER
ACRYLIC RULER

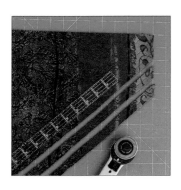

2   Place the quilted fabric on a self-
    healing cutting mat. Using a rotary
    cutter and acrylic ruler, cut between
    the rows of stitching through all layers
    of fabric.

3   Stitch the fabric strips to the base fabric,
    using the previous stitching line as a
    guide.

4   Seam, bind, or finish the raw edges of
    the base fabric.

5   Machine wash and dry the fabric.

❖ IF THE STRIP IS TOO SHORT to cover the desired design, make a perpendicular cut
   across the end of the strip. Overlap the cut
   end with another strip, and continue stitching. After washing, the join will be hidden.

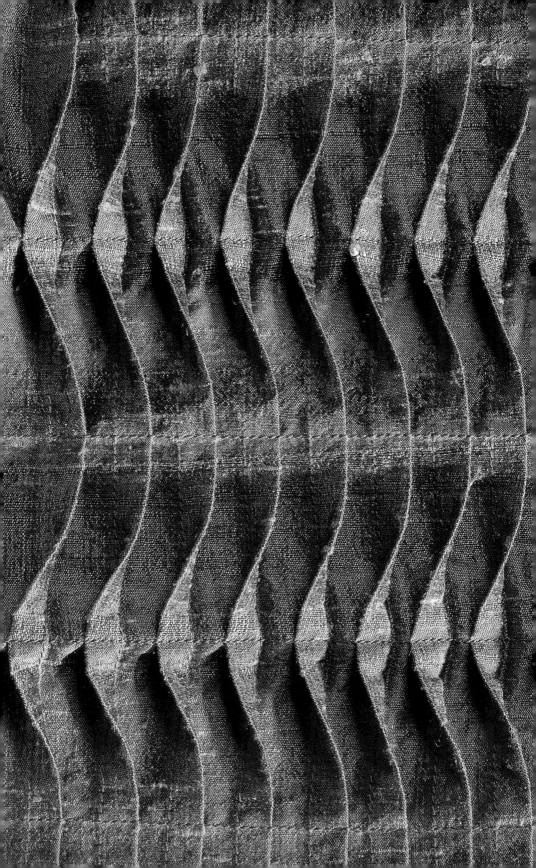

Tucks

TUCKS ARE FOLDS OF FABRIC THAT ARE STITCHED together to create tailored, decorative effects or shaping. The width of the tucks and the space between the tucks can be adjusted, depending on the project and the finished purpose. Spaced tucks and blind tucks differ in the amount of fabric allowed between the tucks; they can be used on lightweight to medium-weight fabric. Blind tucks meet each other, whereas spaced tucks have a flat area of fabric between them. There are many special kinds of tucks that may be created as variations of blind and spaced tucks. Cross tucks are stitched at right angles to one another, and Mexican tucks are pressed in alternate directions and stitched in place. Both create dimension and texture. Pintucks and shell tucks are small and delicate and work best with lightweight fabrics.

Blind Tucks

EASY

SUPPLIES

CHALK MARKER
RULER
PRESS CLOTH

1 Determine the desired finished width of the tucks.

2 Cut the fabric larger than the desired finished size. The size will vary, depending on the width of the tucks and the number you use. Practice on a sample before starting your project.

3 With the right side of the fabric up, mark the stitching lines of the tucks parallel to the grainline using a chalk marker and ruler. Each tuck requires two stitching lines spaced twice the distance of the finished tuck width. The tucks are spaced at the same distance that they are wide. For example, if the finished width of the tuck is $\frac{1}{2}$ in., the pairs of stitching lines will be I in. apart and spaced $\frac{1}{2}$ in. from each other.

Example

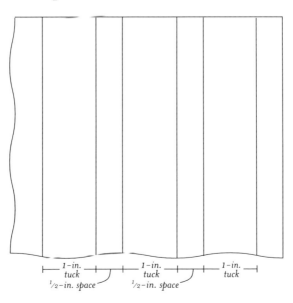

1-in. tuck $\frac{1}{2}$-in. space   1-in. tuck $\frac{1}{2}$-in. space   1-in. tuck

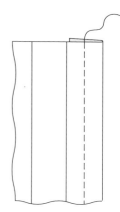

4　Fold the fabric with the wrong sides together, matching the first pair of stitching lines. Pin the tuck in place. Stitch along the marked lines.

5　Repeat until all tucks have been stitched.

6　Using a press cloth over the fabric, press each tuck flat after it is stitched.

7　With the fabric flat and right side up, press all the tucks in the same direction. Staystitch across the ends if necessary.

❖ **EXPERIMENT WITH PRACTICAL or decorative stitches when creating tucks.**

Spaced Tucks

EASY

1 Determine the desired finished width of the tucks and
the space between tucks.

2 Cut the fabric larger than the desired finished size. The size will
vary, depending on the width of the tucks and the number you use.
Practice on a sample before starting your project.

3 With the right side of the fabric up, mark the stitching lines of the
tucks parallel to the grainline using a chalk marker and ruler. Each
tuck requires two stitching lines spaced twice the distance of the
finished tuck width. To determine the distance between the pairs of
stitching lines, add the width of the finished tuck to the space
between the tucks. For example, if the finished tuck width is $\frac{1}{2}$ in.
and the spacing between tucks is $\frac{1}{2}$ in., then the pairs of stitching
lines will be 1 in. apart and spaced 1 in. from each other.

Example

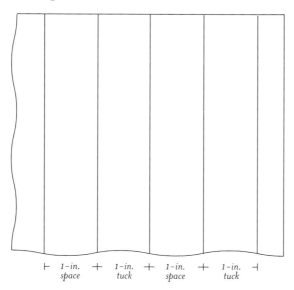

| 1-in. | 1-in. | 1-in. | 1-in. |
| space | tuck | space | tuck |

4 Fold the fabric with the wrong sides together, matching the first pair of stitching lines. Pin the tuck in place. Stitch along the marked lines.

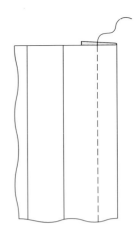

5 Follow Steps 5 to 7 for "Blind Tucks."

VARIATIONS

◆ For Mexican tucks, follow the instructions for spaced tucks, omitting the second pressing. Press the pleats flat in one direction. Stitch a perpendicular line across the pleats approximately every 3 in. Rotate the fabric, and stitch the tucks down in the opposite direction between the previous stitching lines.

◆ For cross tucks, follow the instructions for spaced tucks, omitting the staystitching. Rotate the fabric so that first set of tucks face down. Repeat the process, forming perpendicular tucks on the crosswise grain.

Corded Tucks

INTERMEDIATE

SUPPLIES

RATTAIL OR CORDING
CHALK MARKER
RULER
ZIPPER FOOT

1   Determine the desired space between the tucks.

2   Cut the fabric larger than the desired finished size. The size will vary, depending on the width of the tucks and the number you use. Practice on a sample before starting your project.

3   Wrap the fabric around the cord, and pin it close to the cord.

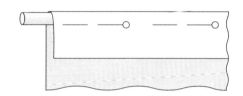

4   Remove the cord, and measure the width of the tuck. With the right side of the fabric up, mark the stitching lines of the tucks parallel to the grainline using a chalk marker. Each tuck requires two stitching lines spaced the distance determined by measuring the finished tuck width. To determine the distance between the pairs of stitching lines, add the width of the finished tuck to the space between the tucks. For example, if the finished tuck width is ⅛ in. and the spacing between tucks is ½ in., then the pairs of stitching lines will be ¼ in. apart and spaced ⅝ in. from each other.

5   Fold the fabric with the wrong sides together around the cording, and match the first pair of stitching lines. Pin in place.

6   Place the zipper foot in the sewing machine. Adjust the needle position to the left. Stitch close to the cord.

7   Continue stitching until all tucks have been stitched.

Pintucks

INTERMEDIATE

❖ A SEVEN-GROOVE PINTUCK FOOT is a good size
for most projects.

❖ THE FABRIC WEIGHT is the determining factor
for the size of the twin needle. The finer the
fabric, the closer the space between the twin
needles and the smaller the needle size.

❖ INCREASING THE NEEDLE TENSION or inserting
gimp cord will raise the pintucks.

1 Cut the fabric larger than the desired finished size. The size will vary, depending on the width of the tucks and the number you use. Practice on a sample before starting your project.

SUPPLIES

PINTUCK FOOT
TWIN NEEDLE
COTTON EMBROIDERY THREAD

2 With the right side of the fabric up, mark the stitching line of the first pintuck parallel to the grainline by pulling a thread or pressing a crease.

3 Place the pintuck foot and twin needle in the sewing machine. The sample in the photos was done with a five-groove pintuck foot and a 2.0/80 needle. Thread each needle with cotton embroidery thread, and fill the bobbin with the same thread. The threads should not cross each other at any point.

4 Set the machine for a 2-mm-long straight stitch. Stitch the first pintuck row along the marked line.

5 Continue stitching rows as desired. Guide the adjacent pintucks under the grooves in the foot to maintain an evenly spaced parallel lines of stitching.

Shell Tucks or Edging

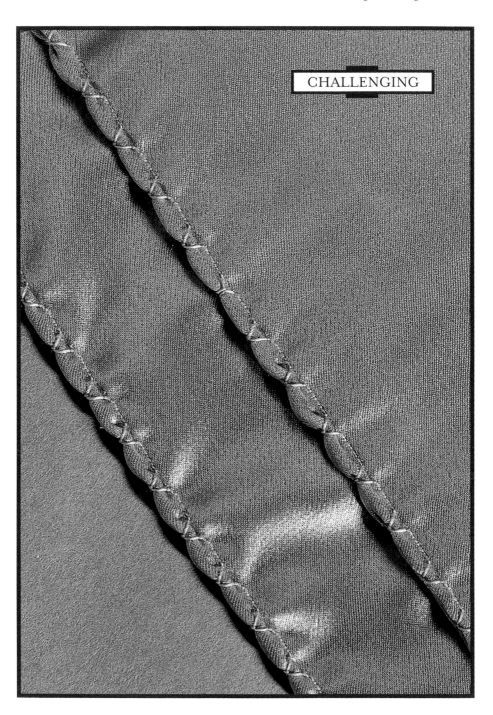

1 Stitch a ⅛-in.-wide spaced
tuck or a ⅛-in. hem in the
fabric.

SUPPLIES

EMBROIDERY FOOT

EMBROIDERY THREAD

2 Place the embroidery foot in the sewing machine. Set the machine
for a 3.5-mm- to 4.5-mm-wide by 1.5-mm-long blindstitch.
Tighten the needle tension slightly if necessary. Thread the needle
with embroidery thread.

3 With the wrong side up, place the
tuck or hem under the foot so that
the zigzag of the stitch gathers the
folded edge into a scallop. Make a
sample before beginning your project. Adjust the stitch settings as necessary. Each scallop should be
approximately ⅜ in. long.

4 Continue stitching until all the tucks have been stitched.

❖ TIGHTEN THE NEEDLE TENSION **if the scallop is not being gathered enough. Loosen
the tension if the fabric is puckering.**

❖ USE AS A DECORATIVE HEM FINISH **on baby
or lingerie items.**

CHAPTER 19

Weaving

WEAVING IS A PROCESS OF INTERLACING STRIPS OF FABRIC, ribbon, or trim to create a new fabric. Woven pieces are held together by fusing a piece of iron-on interfacing to the wrong side and basting along the outside edges. A variety of effects are possible by altering the sequence of the weave, by mixing and layering the elements, and by choosing a variety of fabrics. Weaving results in a fairly crisp fabric that is best used only as an accent, such as on a garment collar, cuffs, and pockets. It is also an excellent technique for creating unique home decorating accessories, including pillow tops, table runners, and Christmas stockings. Beads or buttons can be applied to the finished weaving for added embellishment.

Plain Weave with Ribbon

INTERMEDIATE

SUPPLIES

FUSIBLE INTERFACING

PADDED WORK SURFACE OR PIN
    WEAVING BOARD

RIBBONS

BODKIN

PRESS CLOTH

1   Determine the desired finished size of the weaving.

2   Determine the amount of ribbon needed. To do this, make a sample of one repeat and multiply by the total number of repeats. Add extra for take up and seam allowances.

3   Cut a piece of fusible interfacing the size of the finished weaving plus ½ in. for the seam allowance.

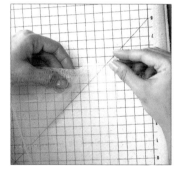

4   Pin the interfacing glue side up onto a padded work surface.

5   Cut the ribbons into the lengths needed, including seam allowances.

6   Position half the ribbon strips right side up on top of the interfacing. Begin at the left edge, and arrange the ribbons vertically and parallel to one another.

7   Secure the top and bottom of the ribbons with pins.

8   Attach a bodkin to one end of one ribbon strip. Beginning at one vertical edge, weave the ribbon horizontally through the secured ribbons. Pass over the first ribbon, under the second ribbon, over the third ribbon, and so on.

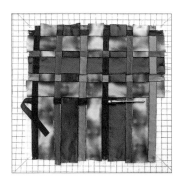

9   Attach the bodkin to one end of another ribbon strip, and repeat the process, going under the first vertical ribbon, over the second, under the third, and so on.

10   Continue weaving until the design is complete.

11   Secure the left and right edges of the weaving with pins.

12   Square up the ribbons, eliminating any gaps or spaces.

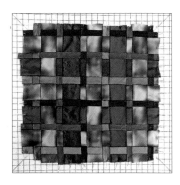

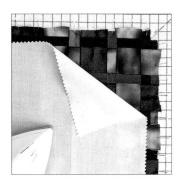

13   Place a press cloth on top of the weaving; and fuse the interfacing in place, following the manufacturer's instructions.

14   Remove the weaving from the padded surface. Using a straight stitch, machine stitch just inside the outer edges to secure the ends.

VARIATIONS

◆ Try a zigzag weave with ribbons.

◆ Add decorative topstitching.

◆ Use woven and knotted fabric tubes.

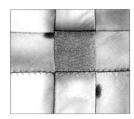

Materials

SELECTING APPROPRIATE MATERIALS IS OFTEN THE MOST IMPORTANT FACTOR IN determining the success of a project. Make samples and experiment with a variety of supplies to come up with the best combination. Some techniques require very exact tools, others may vary, depending on the fabric, purpose, or size. The supply lists given in the text provide starting points. Adjust and substitute as you gain skill and confidence.

THREADS

Use quality threads for best results. Select thread that is appropriate to the technique and the fabric. A wide variety of decorative threads are now available, offering unlimited embellishment possibilities.

Threads are manufactured in a variety of weights; the higher the number, the finer the thread. Needle size should correspond to thread weight; heavier and metallic threads require needles with larger eyes. Thread should always be wound onto an empty bobbin, do not "layer" threads.

BOBBIN THREAD

A very fine 60- or 70-weight polyester or nylon thread, generally available in white and black. Use with decorative stitching to prevent threads from bunching up under the fabric. Many manufacturers produce extra-large economy spools.

COTTON EMBROIDERY THREAD

Ideal for decorative stitching and seaming fine, delicate fabrics. Produced by many manufacturers in a 60-weight variety in a wide range of colors.

GIMP

A heavy, cordlike thread, generally available in black and white. Use for machine gathering and corded pintucks.

MERCERIZED COTTON THREAD

A low-sheen, versatile thread with less strength and stretch than polyester. It is available in a variety of weights and colors. Use for seaming natural-fiber fabrics and for decorative stitching.

METALLIC THREAD

Metallic threads add sparkle to machine embellishments. They are fragile and tend to fray and/or break. A special metallic needle is recommended for sewing, and tension may need to be adjusted.

MONOFILAMENT THREAD

A transparent thread available in clear for light-colored fabrics and smoke for dark-colored fabrics. Use with couching, appliqué, or quilting for invisible stitches.

PEARL COTTON OR RAYON

A heavy, twisted, decorative thread available in a variety of weights and colors. Recommended for bobbin work or couching.

POLYESTER UNIVERSAL THREAD

A strong, fade-resistant thread with some stretch. Look for long-staple varieties, which provide the best results. Generally recommended for seaming non-natural fabrics and knits.

RAYON THREAD

Used only for decorative stitching, it has a silk-like luster and comes in 30- and 40-weight varieties. It is available in a wide range of beautiful solid and variegated colors.

RIBBON FLOSS

A flat, very narrow, braided rayon ribbon. Use for decorative bobbin work and couching. A fragile thread that does not withstand a lot of wear.

SILK THREAD

A lustrous, strong thread that's wonderful for basting, beading, decorative stitching, and seaming silk fabrics.

TOPSTITCHING THREAD

A heavy, tightly twisted, 30-weight thread used for decorative topstitching, corded buttonholes, and machine gathering.

NEEDLES

Select needles to match the fabric and thread. Machine needles are labeled with two numbers, which refer to the shaft diameter. The first number (60 to 120) is the European size; the second number (8 to 21) is the American size. Larger needles are designated by a higher number. Hand-sewing needles are the opposite: The needle size gets smaller as the number increases. Always begin a machine sewing project with a new needle.

MACHINE NEEDLES

DOUBLE WING NEEDLE

A variation of a twin needle that has one universal needle and one wing needle. This needle is used with zigzag-capable machines only to create decorative hemstitching.

EMBROIDERY OR METALLIC NEEDLE

Specially designed with a large eye for sewing with decorative and metallic threads. Available in a variety of sizes.

HEMSTITCHING OR WING NEEDLE

Wing needles have metal extensions on two sides that separate the fabric fibers and produce a small hole. They are available in sizes 100/16 and 120/19 and are most often used to create heirloom stitching.

MICROTEX OR SHARP NEEDLE

A thin needle with a sharp point that produces smooth seams. Use for sewing on densely woven fabric and for heirloom sewing.

TWIN OR DOUBLE NEEDLE

A twin needle has two universal needles attached with a cross bar onto a single shank, which creates parallel lines of stitching. Size is designated by two numbers. The first number (1.6 to 8.0) indicates the distance between the needles. The higher the number, the bigger the space. The second number (70 to 100) is the size of the needles. Use with zigzag-capable machines for topstitching, decorative stitching, and pintucks.

UNIVERSAL NEEDLE

This needle is available in many sizes and can be used for most sewing projects.

HAND-SEWING NEEDLES

BEADING NEEDLE

Long, very fine needle specially designed for working with beads. Select the size to correspond with the opening in the beads and the fabric weight.

SHARPS

The most common type of hand-sewing needle, they are available in a variety of sizes.

STABILIZERS

Most machine embellishment techniques benefit from the use of some type of stabilizer. They provide temporary or permanent support to the fabric, preventing puckering and distortion. Select a stabilizer appropriate for the process and the fabric. Always test before beginning a project.

EMBROIDERY HOOPS

The simplest stabilizer to use. They are available in a variety of materials and sizes and hold the fabric taut and flat for stitching.

FUSIBLE INTERFACING

Iron-on fusible interfacing, available in a variety of weights, provides body and adds permanent stability to projects. Always test before using. Interfacing can be used in conjunction with other temporary stabilizers.

HEAT-AWAY STABILIZER

A loosely woven, chemically treated stabilizer that disintegrates when heated with a dry iron. Use with fabrics that cannot be washed or do not have dense decorative stitching. Follow the manufacturer's guidelines for heating, to avoid scorching fabrics.

TEAR-AWAY STABILIZER

Paperlike stabilizer sold repackaged or by the yard. Use with medium-weight to heavyweight fabrics that have dense stitching. This stabilizer may leave a whisker-like residue after it is removed. It can be used in layers for extra stability and can be cut instead of torn away to prevent stitch distortion.

WATER-SOLUBLE STABILIZER

This stabilizer is available as a spray-on and brush-on stiffener and in clear gel sheets. Multiple applications or layers may be used for added stability. Excellent for use with fine or delicate fabrics. Prewash all fabrics before beginning. When complete, dissolve in water, following the manufacturer's instructions.

MACHINE FEET

Specialty sewing-machine feet allow for faster and more accurate results. Many have multiple uses to create a variety of embellishments. Check with your local machine dealer for information.

BRAIDING OR CORDING FOOT

This foot has single or multiple grooves to guide decorative threads.

CORDONNET FOOT

This foot has a single small hole to guide heavier thread for gathering or couching.

DARNING FOOT

Use this foot for free-motion embroidery or for darning when the feed dogs are down.

EMBROIDERY FOOT

The bottom of this foot has a large open groove to accommodate wide stitching. It is also available in clear and open-toe varieties.

LEATHER-ROLLER FOOT

This foot guides the fabric with a large metal wheel. Excellent for sewing leather and suede and for creating large piping.

PINTUCK FOOT

The bottom of this foot has between three and nine grooves for guiding pintucks.

TAILOR TACK FOOT

This foot has a raised bar down the center over which zigzag loops are stitched. It is use to form tailor tacks or short fringe.

WALKING FOOT

This foot is a large machine attachment that provides additional feed dogs on top of the fabric. Use when sewing slippery fabrics, fabrics with pile, or multiple layers of fabric.

ZIPPER FOOT

A narrow foot with needle cutouts on either side. Use for inserting zippers and for creating piping.

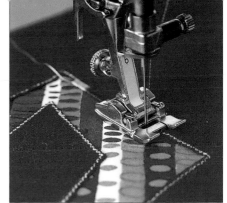

Sources

Clotilde, Inc.
B 3000
Louisiana, MO 63353-3000
(800) 772-2891
Marking tools and notions.
Catalog available.

Dharma Trading Co.
P.O. Box 150916
San Rafael, CA 94915
(415) 456-7657
(800) 542-5227
Dyes, paints, and related products. Catalog available.

Diane Ericson/ReVisions
P.O. Box 7404
Carmel, CA 93921
Stencils. Catalog available.

Hot Potatoes
209 Tenth Ave. S.
Suite 311
Nashville, TN 37203
(615) 255-4055
Rubber fabric stamps.
Catalog available.

Ornamental Resources
P.O. Box 3010
1427 Miner St.
Idaho Springs, CO 80452
(303) 279-2102
(800) 876-6762
Beads, findings, etc.
Catalog available.

Silkpaint Corp.
P.O. Box 18
Waldon, MD 64092
(816) 891-7774
Fiber-Etch and fabrics
for devoré.

Things Japanese
9805 N.E. 116th St., Suite 7160
Kirkland, WA 98034-4248
(206) 821-2287
Silk thread and metallic fabric
paint. Catalog available.

Speed Stitch
3113-D Broadpoint Dr.
Harbor Heights, FL 33983
(800) 874-4115
Sulky products, specialty threads,
and stabilizers. Catalog available.

Web of Thread
1410 Broadway
Paducah, KY 42001
(502) 575-9700
(800) 955-8185
Specialty threads and ribbons.

Thai Silks
252 State St.
Los Altos, CA 94022
(800) 722-7455
Silk fabrics and rayon-and-silk
velvet. Swatches available for a
small fee.

The Yarn Collection
234 Strawberry Village
Mill Valley, CA 94941
(800) 908-9276
Specialty yarns, ribbons,
and trims.